STORIES THAT FEED YOUR SOUL

STORIES
THAT FEED YOUR
SOUL

TONY
CAMPOLO

BESTSELLING AUTHOR OF *LET ME TELL YOU A STORY*

Regal

From Gospel Light
Ventura, California, U.S.A.

Published by Regal
From Gospel Light
Ventura, California, U.S.A.
Printed in the U.S.A.

ISBN 978-0-8307-4775-7

Rights for publishing this book outside the U.S.A. or in non-English languages are
administered by Gospel Light Worldwide, an international not-for-profit ministry.
For additional information, please visit www.glww.org, email info@glww.org, or write
to Gospel Light Worldwide, 1957 Eastman Avenue, Ventura, CA 93003, U.S.A.

Dedicated to Joel Kent Holland:
a man of integrity,
and a brother-in-law
who loves God and
loves his family.

CONTENTS

PART 5: LIVING WITH HOPE

PART 6: PRAYING IN THE SPIRIT

PART 7: GOD'S PLAN FOR US

PART 8: THE ASSURANCE WE NEED

INTRODUCTION

"The gospel is seldom heard. It is overheard," said Søren Kierkegaard, the Danish existentialist philosopher and theologian.

Kierkegaard compared reading the Bible to the way in which you might overhear a conversation. He asks you to imagine standing behind two men on a street corner, while waiting for a break in the traffic so you can cross the street. The men are talking about someone—and then, suddenly, you realize they are talking about you. You listen intently, because what they are saying is both critical and revealing about who you are. So it is with the reading of Scripture. As you read the stories and conversations recorded in the Bible thousands of years ago, you are likely to become aware that what is being said has been written about you. While you are not being addressed directly, the words, nevertheless, seem to deal with *your* struggles, *your* needs, *your* questions, and *your* hopes. Sometimes, what is overheard can be quite disturbing.

Within the Bible itself, we find stories of people who overhear things that at first seem to be about others, only to realize that they themselves are being described. As a case in point, this is what happened to David, Israel's most notable king. Through a story, told to him by Nathan the prophet, David is forced to face up to a dark side of himself and the horrible evil he had done to a beautiful woman and her innocent husband (see 2 Sam. 12:1-7).

One day, King David looked down from the roof of his palace and saw a woman named Bathsheba washing herself. David lusted after her and decided to translate his lusts into action and to "have" Bathsheba for himself. Bathsheba was already married, and her husband, Uriah, one of Israel's generals, was away with the army, at war. To make a long story very short, David slept with Bathsheba and, when the king knew she had become pregnant, he arranged to have Uriah placed at the front of the battle so that he was certain to be killed. Once Uriah was out of the way, David made Bathsheba his own wife.

To Nathan, God's prophet, fell the task of forcing David to face up to the enormity of his evil. Nathan did not condemn the king directly, but chose instead the indirect method of telling David a story that would force him to condemn himself. This is the story:

A certain rich man owned a large herd of sheep and possessed all the good things that a wealthy man might enjoy. Nevertheless, when this rich man had a visitor for dinner, he took the beloved lamb of a poor neighbor—a lamb that was loved like a child. He killed the lamb and served it for dinner, leaving the poor farmer heartbroken.

King David was outraged by the story Nathan told him and demanded that the greedy rich man be brought to justice and severely punished. Only then, when Nathan pointed his finger at the king and said, "Thou art the man!" (*KJV*), did David realize that the story was really about himself, and end up judging and condemning himself. Nathan's story was, as Kierkegaard would say, the "indirect method" by which David "overheard" the horror of the kind of person he had become.

Overhearing the *Whole* Gospel

Most of us realize that there is both an objective and a subjective side to becoming a Christian. On the one hand, we accept a need for "sound doctrine." We recognize that our faith must be built on solid propositional truths. On the other hand, however, we sense that there is a need for a personal (subjective) and transforming encounter with the resurrected and ever-present Christ.

When it comes to propositional truth, I believe there is no better statement of the doctrines that are essential for a Christian to believe than the Apostles' Creed. In this creed, we find a brief, but comprehensive, survey of the teachings that have historically defined the Christian faith. The Apostles' Creed goes back more than 1,500 years.

Sound doctrine, most of us realize, is not enough. Becoming a Christian involves something more than simply saying yes to a list of biblically prescribed propositional truths. If giving intellectual assent to the fact that Jesus died on the cross for our sins would provide believers with salvation, then Satan would be "saved." James 2:19 tells us that "even the demons believe—and tremble!" (*NKJV*). That "something more" that is necessary for salvation comes from subjectively surrendering to God. It requires a yielding to the changes that God wants to effect in our lives. It involves becoming emotionally, psychologically and spiritually open to the transformations that the eighth chapter of Romans describes as the work of the Holy Spirit (*NLT*).

Evangelicals believe that Jesus waits at the door of the innermost recesses of our being, saying, "Behold, I stand at the door, and knock" (Rev. 3:20, *KJV*) and that He longs for each of us to make the existential decision to open ourselves up to what He wants to do in our lives.

Jesus the Storyteller

Two thousand years ago, Jesus told stories in order to help His disciples and other listeners more fully understand His teachings. The parables of Jesus were used to make clear many of the theological truths He wanted His disciples to grasp. For instance, when seeking to convey what He wanted them to know about the future of the world, Jesus told His disciples the parable of the wheat and the tares:

> The kingdom of heaven may be compared to someone who sowed good seed in his field; but while everybody was asleep, an enemy came and sowed weeds among the wheat, and then went away. So when the plants came up and bore grain, then the weeds appeared as well. And the slaves of the householder came and said to him, "Master, did you not sow good seed in your field? Where, then, did these weeds come from?" He answered, "An enemy has done this." The slaves said to him, "Then do you want us to go and gather them?" But he replied, "No; for in gathering the weeds you would uproot the wheat along with them.

Let both of them grow together until the harvest; and at
harvest time I will tell the reapers, 'Collect the weeds first
and bind them in bundles to be burned, but gather the
wheat into my barn'" (Matt. 13:24-30).

Many Bible teachers believe that wheat, which Jesus talked
about in this story, symbolizes the kingdom of God, and that the
tares represent the kingdom of evil. In this parable, Jesus made it
clear that the future would be marked both by increasing evil in
the world and by the growing presence of His Father's kingdom.
Both kingdoms would grow in size and significance until that
time when human history would climax with the harvest and the
simultaneous destruction of the evil kingdom.

As a boy, I can remember sitting in church during a Sunday
evening service and hearing the preacher go on and on about how
the world was becoming more and more decadent with every passing day. He declared that everything about this world was in a
downward spiral, and then he went on to support his case with sta-
tistics that demonstrated how divorce and abortions were on the
increase, how pornography was no longer confined to "sex shops,"
and how crime had become a societal epidemic. As the preacher
went on and on, sounding like a prophet of doom, an elderly
woman seated directly behind me kept on saying, "Hallelujah!
Thank You, Jesus!" and "Yes! Yes!"

When I asked my mother why all the bad news was making
this woman so happy, she explained that these "bad things" were
evidence for this lady that the second coming of Christ was at
hand. She told me that this woman believed that the increasing of
evil in the world meant that Jesus would have to return soon in
order to bring it to an end.

Of course, there is some truth in what that church lady was
affirming. Satan's kingdom (that is, the tares) *is* more and more evident in this world with every passing day. It seems apparent that
evil is ever more pervasive and powerful. Just watching the evening
news on television provides ample evidence to buttress the percep-
tion that the kingdom of evil is constantly increasing. *But*, in the

face of this reality, we should not lose sight of all the evidence that the kingdom of God is also asserting itself around the globe. Alongside the kingdom of evil, the wheat, which symbolizes the kingdom of God, is also growing in size and significance. It is crucial for us to stop and consider that while decadence might be seen to be the order of the day here in America, there are glowing reports of how the church is growing exponentially in places such as China. In the midst of all that is so very wrong in the world, we must not ignore the revivals that are bringing hundreds of thousands to Christ weekly in cities and villages throughout Africa and Latin America, or the church growth in Korea that is nothing short of phenomenal.

Those prophets of doom err when they do not recognize the many positive signs of the coming of the kingdom of God. Consider these facts:

- In 1980—70 percent of the world's population was illiterate. Today that number is 20 percent.
- In 1980—50 percent of the world's population suffered from malnutrition. Today that number is 25 percent.
- In 1980—One in four children died in the first year of life. Today that number is one in eight.
- In the nineteenth century—small pox killed five hundred million people. Today smallpox is nearly eradicated.
- Polio and Hansen's disease have been dramatically cut.

On the one hand, the parable of the wheat and the tares keeps us from becoming as overly optimistic about the future as those old-time liberal "social gospelers," who preached that humanity would simply evolve into a Utopian society. On the other hand, this story keeps us from becoming as pessimistic about the future as that preacher I heard as a boy, who saw nothing good happening in this world.

The message of Jesus in this parable is more balanced than either of those extreme points of view. In this simple story, He set forth an eschatology that sophisticated theologians would likely

take volumes to explain. Jesus gave us profound truths about the
future in a form that is easy for us to understand. He told us a story.

Exploring Subjective Receptivity

In addition to using parables to explain the objective truths of what
God's kingdom is all about and how it unfolds in history, Jesus also
used a variety of stories and analogies to help us understand that
which we must experience subjectively if we are to be "born again."
In a story describing one of the most memorable of His personal
encounters, we learn about the mystical dimensions of having a
right relationship with God. In John 3, Jesus lets us know that there
is something that must take place inwardly (as Kierkegaard would
say) if we are to experience the kind of subjective transformation required of those who would be part of His kingdom.

> Now there was a Pharisee named Nicodemus, a leader of
> the Jews. He came to Jesus by night and said to him,
> "Rabbi, we know that you are a teacher who has come
> from God; for no one can do these signs that you do apart
> from the presence of God." Jesus answered him, "Very
> truly, I tell you, no one can see the kingdom of God with-
> out being born from above." Nicodemus said to him,
> "How can anyone be born after having grown old? Can
> one enter a second time into the mother's womb and be
> born?" Jesus answered, "Very truly, I tell you, no one can
> enter the kingdom of God without being born of water
> and Spirit. What is born of the flesh is flesh, and what is
> born of the Spirit is spirit. Do not be astonished that I said
> to you, 'You must be born from above.' The wind blows
> where it chooses, and you hear the sound of it, but you do
> not know where it comes from or where it goes. So it is
> with everyone who is born of the Spirit" (John 3:1-8).

In another of His parables, Jesus brilliantly described a variety
of subjective responses from those who hear the gospel. I am refer-

ring to the familiar parable of the sower. In this parable, Jesus tells His listeners:

> Listen! A sower went out to sow. And as he sowed, some seeds fell on the path, and the birds came and ate them up. Other seeds fell on rocky ground, where they did not have much soil, and they sprang up quickly, since they had no depth of soil. But when the sun rose, they were scorched; and since they had no root, they withered away. Other seeds fell among thorns, and the thorns grew up and choked them. Other seeds fell on good soil and brought forth grain, some a hundredfold, some sixty, some thirty. Let anyone with ears listen (Matt. 13:3-9)!

This is the only parable after which Jesus provided an explanation for His disciples. Realizing that they hadn't understood its full meaning, He told them:

> When anyone hears the word of the kingdom and does not understand it, the evil one comes and snatches away what is sown in the heart; this is what was sown on the path. As for what was sown on rocky ground, this is the one who hears the word and immediately receives it with joy; yet such a person has no root, but endures only for a while, and when trouble or persecution arises on account of the word, that person immediately falls away. As for what was sown among thorns, this is the one who hears the word, but the cares of the world and the lure of wealth choke the word, and it yields nothing. But as for what was sown on good soil, this is the one who hears the word and understands it, who indeed bears fruit and yields, in one case a hundredfold, in another sixty, and in another thirty (Matt. 13:19-23).

While none of us will achieve the effectiveness in storytelling exemplified by Jesus, He made it clear that the telling of stories is a very useful, if not essential, tool for any communicator. Those of us who are called to be preachers and teachers in today's world would do well to emulate the Master Communicator as we strive to make the gospel clear and interesting to our listeners.

Finally, it is my hope that all who read the stories I have gathered here will gain some further insights into what is involved in becoming a Christian, and how we as Christians are to live out our faith.

The Structuring of the Stories

Rather than giving you these stories in an arbitrary arrangement, I have chosen to organize them in accord with the contents of one specific chapter of the Bible—the eighth chapter of Romans. This particular chapter is one of my favorites and over the years its verses have provided me with more texts for sermons than any other section of Scripture. It is a chapter that, for me, addresses almost all the components of a holistic theology.

I have found, in the eighth chapter of Romans, eight distinct themes. These themes suggested for me the outline and chapter titles for this book. No doubt, more proficient biblical scholars can discover more themes than those I have listed, but I am hopeful that these will provide some order to the stories that follow.

1. Freedom from Condemnation (vv. 1-4)
2. The New Life in Christ (vv. 5-14)
3. Intimacy with God (vv. 15-17)
4. The Call to Rescue Creation (vv. 18-23)
5. Living with Hope (vv. 24-25)
6. Praying in the Spirit (vv. 26-27)
7. God's Plan for Us (vv. 28-30)
8. The Assurance We Need (vv. 31-39)

Now that you know where I'm going in this book, let me tell you a story that will feed your soul. Better still, let me tell you an array of stories that will help you as you try to tell the greatest story ever told.

Tony Campolo

PART I

FREEDOM FROM CONDEMNATION

PART I

FREEDOM FROM CONDEMNATION

There is therefore now no condemnation for those who are
in Christ Jesus. For the law of the Spirit of life in Christ Jesus has set you
free from the law of sin and of death. For God has done what the law,
weakened by the flesh, could not do: by sending his own Son in the like-
ness of sinful flesh, and to deal with sin, he condemned sin in the flesh, so
that the just requirement of the law might be fulfilled in us, who walk not
according to the flesh but according to the Spirit.
ROMANS 8:1-4

These verses speak for themselves. They declare clearly and forth-rightly that Jesus did not come into the world to condemn us, but that through Him we can be saved from condemnation. On the cross, He took upon Himself the condemnation that each of us deserves. This is the real Jesus for whom the world is waiting.

1

SOMEBODY STOLE JESUS

A few years ago, I heard a story about something that supposedly happened in St. Louis, Missouri. Apparently someone stole the doll that represented the baby Jesus from the manger scene outside the city hall. The next morning, a television newscaster announced in a somber voice, "Someone has stolen Jesus. Last night someone went to the manger scene at city hall and stole the baby Jesus. This morning, Jesus is missing. If any of you out there have any information about where Jesus might be found, please contact this station immediately. We are most anxious to recover Jesus and put Him back where He belongs."

Whether or not this is a true story, the message is clear. Many people who look at contemporary Christianity and see what we have done with the Jesus of Scripture are asking the question, "Who stole the biblical Jesus? Does anyone know how we can recover Him and restore Him to the place where He belongs?"

Too often, the real Jesus, who is filled with compassion, has been stolen away. There are those who have replaced Him with their made-up Jesus, who offers only harsh judgment on sinners like us.

2

SIN FORGIVEN
AND FORGOTTEN

A man I know in Australia told me the story of a boy who came to see something of the grace of God in his seventh-grade school teacher. Billy had a younger sister who was so severely disabled she could not get out of her wheelchair. When it was time for Annie to go to school, Billy was the one responsible for her. He pushed her wheelchair to school, went to class with his sister, and pushed her from one classroom to the next as the school day unfolded. Caring for his sister never bothered Billy. As a matter of fact, he considered it a privilege to take care of her and took pride in being responsible for her wellbeing.

When Billy was finishing the fourth grade, his sister died and suddenly he was delivered from the responsibility of caring for her. However, instead of being relieved, he became very sad and withdrawn. It was as though the major purpose for his life had been taken from him and he couldn't figure out what to do with himself anymore. It wasn't long before Billy was in all kinds of trouble. Among the schoolteachers, he earned the reputation of being a "bad boy," and during the next few years he seemed to do his best to live up to it.

When Billy entered the seventh grade, he found himself in a class that had a brand-new teacher named Mr. Smith. On the first day of class, Mr. Smith, who had spent a good bit of time looking over the records of the boys and girls in his classroom, called out to Billy.

"Billy, you come up here and sit at this desk right in front of me."

The unhappy boy figured he was in trouble, even though he didn't think he'd done anything wrong on that particular day. He wondered why the teacher was picking on him. Then Mr. Smith spoke again. Picking up the folder that contained Billy's records, he looked at him, and said, "Billy, these records tell me all kinds of bad things about you."

Billy hung his head in shame, but then, to his utter amazement, Mr. Smith tore the folder into little pieces and threw them into the wastebasket. "Billy," he said, "I read over your records and I don't believe a word of what is written there."

It was several days later when the teacher of the Sunday school class of which Billy was a part asked her class a simple question, "Do you know anyone like Jesus?"

Billy smiled as he answered, "I do. Mr. Smith!"

That's not a bad analogy. We have a Jesus who, like that school teacher, destroys the records of our sins and transgressions and presents us to the Father, as it says in the book of Jude, "faultless"!

3

GRACE VERSUS KARMA

One night, on the *Larry King Live* television show, Larry King was interviewing Bono, one of the most famous rock stars in the world.

Bono was talking about his commitment to Christ and how he was trying to live out Christ's love in the world. It was the Christian commitment of this rock star that prompted Larry King to ask an important question.

"What makes Christianity different from all the other religions of the world?" he asked. "What does Christianity have to offer that the other religions do not?"

Bono paused for a moment, then answered, "All the other religions of the world, in one way or another, teach karma. Only Jesus offers grace. In all the other religions of the world, people end up having to pay a penalty for their sins. Only Jesus Christ, by His grace, makes it possible for people to be delivered from the consequences of the sins that they have committed in this life."

After another poignant pause, Bono added, "Sadly, all too often, the church, contrary to Jesus, teaches karma. Most of the time, the church teaches karma instead of offering grace."

4

A FATHER'S FORGIVENESS

Marjorie Kinnan Rawlings's book, *The Yearling*, tells the story of a boy named Jody. He is told by his father that he must destroy his beloved fawn Flag because Flag is doing widespread damage to their farm. In anguish and anger, Jody obeys. He tells his father that he hates him and then, thinking that there is no place for him in the family, he runs away from home. After days of hunger, fatigue and loneliness, he is forced to crawl back home. He is astonished to find that his disappearance has completely disrupted the home and almost killed his grieving father. Jody is overwhelmed. He was wanted, actually wanted!

Gordon Brownville, a preacher friend now gone on to be with the Lord, used to tell the story of how, as a boy, he had been involved in taking, without permission, a neighbor's automobile, only to have the automobile stolen one time while left unattended. The neighbor insisted on having him arrested. The boy's father, who was on a business trip when he heard of it, hurried home and bailed his son out of jail, paid the neighbor more than double the cost of the car and offered his forgiveness to a boy already overcome with guilt and shame. When Gordon told the story, he always added that the most important thing to him was that his father never mentioned the episode again.

5

GRACE IS LIKE DONUTS

One time I was discussing with a small group of junior high kids those things that were unique about the Christian gospel. I tried to explain to them what grace was all about, then asked what made grace different from mercy and justice.

One boy, with a smile on his face and a glint in his eye, answered by saying, "If a cop pulls you over for speeding and gives you a ticket, that's justice."

"If a cop pulls you over for speeding and gives you a warning, that's mercy."

"But if a cop pulls you over for speeding and gives you a Krispy Kreme donut, that's grace."

Grace is the unexpected good news that, instead of meting out the punishment we deserve, Jesus offers us undeserved and unparalleled blessings.

6

JESUS UNDERSTANDS

The story is told of a woman who, overcome with sorrow, went to St. Francis of Assisi. She explained to the saint that her son had committed suicide and she wondered what Jesus would say to him on the Day of Judgment.

St. Francis responded by saying to the woman, "Perhaps Jesus would put His arm around your boy and say, 'I understand. It was hard for Me when I was down there too. They make life very difficult for Christians like you and Me.'"

7

IT WAS MEANT FOR YOU

I don't remember much about my father. I wish I remembered
more. He was a quiet man and said very little, but there was one
time he spoke and his words made a profound impression on me
that has lasted to this day.

I remember sitting in church with my father on a commun-
ion Sunday. The pastor had preached a sermon on the Bible verse
in which the apostle Paul writes, "Therefore whoever eats this
bread or drinks this cup of the Lord in an unworthy manner will
be guilty of the body and blood of the Lord" (1 Cor. 11:27, *NKJV*).
As the sermon wound down, a young woman in her late teens, in
the row in front of us, began to cry. Her body shook as she wept.
Obviously, the sermon had gotten to her. Evidently there was some
sin in her life that made her feel unworthy of the body and the
blood of Christ. As the tray with the bread representing the body
of our Lord was passed to her, she waved it off and continued to
weep. It was at that point that my father put his hand on her
shoulder and, in his broken English and heavy Italian accent, said
gruffly, "Take it, girl! It was meant for you!"

The young woman pulled herself together, took the bread, and
later drank of the cup. I had a sense that my father's declaration
had overridden the sermon and made that young woman aware
that, even though there was sin in her life, there was a Jesus full of
grace who was willing to accept her and love her even though she
was unworthy. I learned something of the grace of God that Sunday and, over the many years since then, I have become even more
aware that Jesus gives Himself to us "while we are yet in our sin,"
and delivers us into a reconciled relationship with God. That's
what grace is all about.

8

A FATHER'S BLIND LOVE

An airplane trip I once made from Denver to Colorado Springs made for a good story. It was a short flight of less than half-an-hour.

As I stood waiting to be called to board the plane, there was no escaping a noisy and happy little girl who was bouncing around, clapping her hands, and chanting joyfully, "I'm gonna see Daddy! I'm gonna see Daddy!" She sang that one line over and over again in a most obnoxious way. At first, I tried to smile at the little girl, who was resplendent in a fluffy dress, patent leather shoes, and pigtails, but it became more and more difficult to smile as she continued to jump up and down, letting everyone know the good news that she was going to see her father. After the first ten minutes of this, what once had been cute had become irritating and obnoxious. I was glad when it was time to board the plane.

However, when I took my seat on the airplane, I found that, much to my dismay, the noisy little girl was sitting right across the aisle from me. She continued to clap her hands and announce to all, in a singsong fashion, that she was going to see her daddy.

Because it was a short flight, the flight attendant was only offering cookies and Coca Cola. Every time she passed the happy little girl, the child took a cookie and another Coca Cola. I found it amazing how many cookies and Coca Colas that little girl was able to consume during the short flight.

As the plane approached the airport in Colorado Springs, it went through a thunderstorm, which made for a rough, bouncy ride.

We all know that cookies do not smell bad, nor does Coca Cola smell bad. Therefore, it figures that if you mix cookies and Coca Cola in a sweet little girl with a fluffy dress, patent leather shoes, and pigtails, what comes out should not smell bad.

Such was not the case this time. It wasn't long before there was an eruption, and what came out was the worst smelling vomit imaginable. It was all over the little girl and all over her mother. What made things even worse was that it came out in waves. Every time I thought that the vomiting had come to an end, there would be another eruption and then another.

When the airplane finally touched down, I couldn't wait to get down the aisle and away from the whole smelly mess. As I walked up the connecting corridor and into the airport, I saw a man standing at the end of the walkway, dressed in a white flannel suit, eagerly looking for someone. I just knew who he was, and I lingered behind because I wanted to see the encounter between this elegantly dressed father and little "vomit-face."

What happened next really took me by surprise. The little girl came running up to her father and he got down on one knee and swept her into his arms. She was covered with vomit and she smelled very bad, but it didn't make any difference to him. He had his little girl and that was all that mattered.

9

ANYBODY CAN BE
A CHRISTIAN

My son Bart is a "pied piper" when it comes to teenagers. He can get them to follow him and to do so with great enthusiasm. In his work with inner-city kids, he has been very effective.

Not too long ago, he scheduled a weekend retreat for several hundred inner-city kids from a very tough neighborhood. Bart ran into some last-minute complications that delayed his travel up into the Pocono Mountains where the retreat was being held. Most of the boys were already at the camp and, unfortunately, there were only two counselors on hand.

Bart was doing his best to get there, but he was running very late. In a van full of teenage boys that was loaded down with piles of luggage, he was hurtling up the Northeast Extension of the Pennsylvania Turnpike when he received a phone call that let him know that he was desperately needed at the camp to bring order to the boys. With just two counselors and two hundred excited teenagers, things were getting out of hand. Bart was doing his best to get there quickly when suddenly one of his rear tires blew out.

Bart got the van off to the side of the road, and he and the boys unloaded all the luggage so that they could get to the spare tire. Bart jacked up the van and was changing the tire when the van slipped off the jack and smashed to the pavement. At that point, Bart blurted out a "religious statement that had no theological content." It was several more hours before the group arrived at the retreat.

When the weekend was over and Bart was heading home with his load of campers, the young man sitting next to him said, "It was a great weekend. I decided to become a Christian this weekend and that's really important."

Bart, really pleased with that comment, asked the young man, "What changed you? What caused you to become a Christian?

Was it the speakers or the Bible study programs, or did someone personally talk to you about Jesus?"

"Nah, none of those things," said the young man. "It was when the van fell off the jack and smashed to the ground and you let loose with those words that you shouldn't have said. I figured then, 'If he can be a Christian, anybody can be a Christian.'"

Sometimes Christians present themselves as so unrealistically pious and above human shortcomings that others feel that becoming a Christian is beyond them. Bart did much to change that impression with that particular young man.

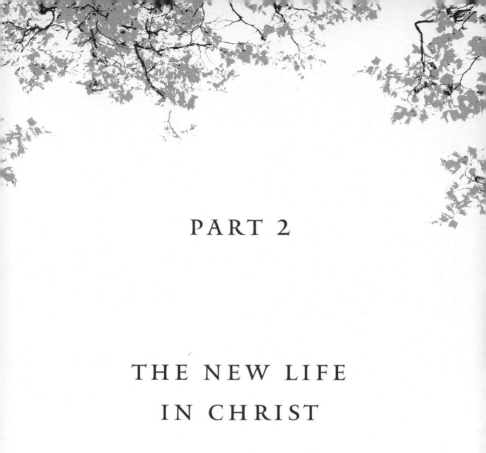

PART 2

THE NEW LIFE
IN CHRIST

PART 2
THE NEW LIFE IN CHRIST

For those who live according to the flesh set their minds on the things of the flesh, but those who live according to the Spirit set their minds on the things of the Spirit. To set the mind on the flesh is death, but to set the mind on the Spirit is life and peace. For this reason the mind that is set on the flesh is hostile to God; it does not submit to God's law—indeed it cannot, and those who are in the flesh cannot please God. But you are not in the flesh; you are in the Spirit, since the Spirit of God dwells in you. Anyone who does not have the Spirit of Christ does not belong to him. But if Christ is in you, though the body is dead because of sin, the Spirit is life because of righteousness. If the Spirit of him who raised Jesus from the dead dwells in you, he who raised Christ from the dead will give life to your mortal bodies also through his Spirit that dwells in you. So then, brothers and sisters, we are debtors, not to the flesh, to live according to the flesh—for if you live according to the flesh, you will die; but if by the Spirit you put to death the deeds of the body, you will live. For all who are led by the Spirit of God are children of God.
ROMANS 8:5-14

Having been recipients of the grace of God, we should realize that, in response, we are expected to live differently. The egoism that has marked our lives must be overcome through the transforming power of the Holy Spirit. How we live should exemplify Christ. His humility, love, joy, trust, compassion, self-giving, and commitment ought to be increasingly evident in the ways we live. We owe Him that, after what He did for us on Calvary.

I

SACRIFICIAL LOVE

I was on a train, leaving the great Victoria Station in London. It was years ago, when they had small separate compartments on the trains. I was in one of them sitting across from two men who looked to be in their late thirties. We were about ten minutes out of the station when one of the men had an epileptic seizure. He slipped off the seat and onto the floor, trembling and shaking. As soon as he slipped off the seat, his friend rolled up a newspaper and inserted it between his teeth to keep him from biting his tongue. When the seizure was over, his friend lifted him up and helped him back onto the seat, took off his own coat and put it around his friend to keep him warm. Then he turned and spoke to me.

"I hope that didn't upset you too much, mister. We never know when these seizures are going to occur, but he hasn't had one for more than two-and-a-half months. We were in Vietnam together. He's British and I'm American. We were both seriously wounded. I lost my leg." He then pulled up his trouser leg and showed me his artificial limb. Then he went on to say, "My friend here had half of his chest torn away by the explosion of a hand grenade. There was shrapnel all through his chest so he couldn't move without feeling excruciating pain. The helicopter that was supposed to come and take us to a hospital was blown out of the air by an enemy rocket, and that seemed to be the end of all of our hopes. It was then that my friend somehow got up on his feet. I don't know how he did it. He reached down and grabbed hold of my shirt and began to pull me through the jungle. Every step was marked by agony. He screamed in pain with every single movement that he made. I yelled at him that he should save himself and that there was no way he was going to get both of us out of the jungle—but somehow he did!"

"A year-and-a-half ago, I found out he had this condition. I sold my condo in New York City and got rid of my car. Then I came over here to be with him because someone has to be with him all the time. As I said, we never know when these seizures are going to hit him. Well, that's our story, mister. Maybe knowing it will make it easier for you to understand the upset you just witnessed."

I looked at this heroic and sacrificial man and said, "Hey, you don't have to apologize to me. I'm a professional speaker. I need stories when I speak, and you have given me one of the best stories I ever heard."

The man answered, "Please don't be impressed. There's nothing to be impressed about. After what he did for me, there isn't anything I wouldn't do for him."

Every Christian should be ready to look at the cross of Jesus and say, "After what He did for me, there isn't anything I wouldn't do for Him."

2
BELIEVING IS NOT ENOUGH

Many years ago, the evangelist J. Edwin Orr was speaking at a university. During the question and answer period following his lecture, a young woman stood and asked, "Isn't it enough just to believe in Jesus? Isn't that what Christianity is all about, simply believing?"

Dr. Orr answered with a question of his own, "Do you believe in marriage?"

"Yes," she replied quickly.

"Why do you believe in marriage?" said Dr. Orr.

"Because it creates a stable relationship that provides security for the partners, and it's a good arrangement in which to raise children. It helps bolster the stability of society," was her answer.

"Good," said Dr. Orr. "I'm a minister of the gospel, so allow me to pronounce you married!"

The young woman laughed and said, "But I haven't yet found a man who will give himself to me and to whom I can give myself. I haven't got a partner with whom I can make a life."

"Exactly," said Dr. Orr. "It's not enough to *believe* in marriage. You have to make a commitment and you have to live out your promise to care for your partner and to do all the things that love requires."

Making a lifetime commitment to live for Christ is at the core of becoming a Christian. Simply believing the truths of the gospel, as important as that is, just isn't enough.

3

SPONTANEOUS GRACE

The director of a very prominent inner-city ministry was driving one of his young workers to a meeting when the young man suddenly shouted, "*Stop!*" When the car stopped, the young man jumped out and ran back to where a derelict-looking man held up a sign that said, "I need money for food." The young Christian worker gave the beggar a five-dollar bill, which was all the money that he was carrying. When he got back into the car, the director of the ministry reprimanded him, "Why did you do that? That guy is probably going to spend the money on drugs or booze. You know that as well as I do."

"You're probably right," the young man answered, "but I gave him the money just in case."

The loving trust and grace, that should mark a Christian, always hopes for the best.

4

RESPONDING TO TERRORISM

My friend Will Willimon was serving as the dean of the chapel at Duke University when the tragedy of 9/11 occurred. Tensions began to run high between Christians, Jews and Muslims on the campus, so Will thought it would be good to have a forum in which a rabbi, an imam, and he, as a Protestant clergyman, could talk about the way in which the respective religions would propose that people respond to the tragedy of that terrorist attack.

The Muslim imam explained that, according to prophet Muhammad, aggression against a Muslim brother should be avenged. The rabbi pointed out that if a Jew were to attack a Muslim, it would be his responsibility to seek punishment—even capital punishment—against the Jew who did that. To all of this, Will Willimon shrugged his shoulders and said, "You two make it very attractive to join either of your religions because that's the way I would want to respond to such evil, but Jesus teaches me to do something that is very much harder. He tells me to love those who would do these evil things and to forgive those who would commit such horrible acts."

Living Christlike is often hard and may, at times, seem unreasonable.

5

ONLY OTHERS
CAN ANSWER

When I was a faculty member at the University of Pennsylvania, I had the opportunity to lead several of my students into a personal relationship with Christ. One young man, who had served as my graduate assistant, had grown up in a completely secular home. He had a wonderful born-again experience and was radically transformed by Christ. One day, as the two of us were walking across campus, a young man from InterVarsity Christian Fellowship, a dynamic Christian student group, saw me and said, "Doctor, we're looking forward to having you speak at our meeting tonight. The meeting starts at seven. Don't be late."

My graduate student immediately asked, "Can I come?"

The young Christian leader, who had confronted us, asked him, "Are you a Christian too?"

To this my assistant responded, "Only *you* can answer that!"

What a fascinating answer. I had never heard that one before. I had always assumed that only the individual could know the truth about whether or not one was a Christian, but in reality my graduate assistant was right. If I really am a Christian, those around me should be able to see that in my life.

6

NOT BLAMING SATAN

Nine-year-old Billy was constantly getting into trouble at school. Every day, little Janey, who sat in front of him in the classroom, complained to the teacher that Billy had been tormenting her.

"He kicks my legs and he pulls my hair, and he's always saying nasty things that really upset me."

One day, in frustration, the teacher, who was one of those people steeped in the language of old-time religion, said, "Billy, did Satan tell you to kick Janey, and get you to pull her hair? Did you let Satan convince you to say those nasty things to her?"

Very quickly, Billy answered, "Well, Satan may have gotten me to kick her and pull her hair, but saying the nasty things was my own idea."

A Christian accepts responsibility for actions; repents when faced with wrongdoing; and then commits to change—with the help of God.

7

THE NEED FOR PASSION

It may be an apocryphal story because I couldn't find a written account of it anywhere, and the university professor who told it to me wasn't sure that it was true, but it's a good story nonetheless. One Sunday, when a young Friedrich Nietzsche, the brilliant atheist existentialist, and his sister were leaving the Lutheran Church pastored by their father, the boy turned, pointed to his father, who stood behind the pulpit, and said bitterly, "Does that *thing* up there ever laugh or cry?"

In later life, Nietzsche would reject Christianity, not because it lacked intellectual credibility, but because it was devoid of passion.

The Spirit-filled Christian is passionate about life and radiates a joyful intensity, even in the midst of what many might call "an ordinary life."

8

LIVING IN A JOYLESS WORLD

I was in an elevator in the Hyatt hotel in Chicago, Illinois. A fellow passenger was a teenager who looked to be about 15 or 16 years of age. He was wearing his pants low in that new "ghetto" style that has become all too common among boys who want to look tough. This kid's trousers were so low that not only could you see underwear protruding above his pants, you could actually see "the crack." I had a tremendous temptation to pull out my pencil and—well, you know—

"How you doing?" I asked, trying to be friendly.

His voice was grumpy as he replied, "All right."

"You having a good day?" I asked him.

"Yeah," he mumbled. There was no joy in this young man.

When we got to the ground floor, the elevator doors did not open. I panicked and began banging on the doors, shouting, "These doors won't open! Will somebody get these doors open? I need to get out of here!"

Then, I heard a voice behind me say, "Sir, the door is open."

As I turned, I realized that this was one of those elevators that had doors on two sides, and I was banging on the wrong doors.

What amazed me was that my fellow passenger didn't laugh. As he started off the elevator, I took hold of his arm, pulled him back, and said, "Hey, kid. Laugh. This is funny!" He couldn't wait to get away from me.

Now, if you are asking me what this has to do with Christianity, let me ask you something: "Did you laugh out loud, or at least chuckle on the inside, when you read about my most embarrassing elevator moment?" Unlike the often joyless world we live in, there is often a joyful hilarity that permeates those who are infused with the Holy Spirit and who know the joy of the Lord.

9

CHURCH CRITICS

Every once in a while, when I am talking to a university student, I get some kind of arrogant response where the student basically says, "I have no time for church; the church is full of hypocrites!"

To that, I always respond, "You are right! That's why you'll feel very much at home if you come and join us. The church is full of hypocrites and, if you'll come, you'll feel just like one of us. There's no doubt that we church people *are* hypocrites. In one way or another, everyone in this world is a hypocrite. It's just that church people, for the most part, are hypocrites who know they are hypocrites and they've come to church to find out how God can help them to overcome their hypocrisy."

Christians love the church and want to be with its people in spite of their shortcomings. Church loyalty is always a part of Christian living.

10

LIVING LIFE TO THE FULLEST

It is said that when Alexander the Great was coming of age, he was told by one of the sages of Athens that it had been prophesied that he would have a choice between living a short but intensely interesting life or a long but boring life. Legend has it that Alexander chose the former over the latter. From my point of view, that was a wise choice.

The Spirit-filled Christian is fully alive and never bored. When being led by God's Spirit, life is an incredible ride.

II

GOD'S JESTER

St. Francis of Assisi often called himself a jester for God. Everywhere he went, he brought joyful vitality to those whom he encountered. He made it clear that true spirituality was to be in a state of joyfulness. Often he would pick up a stick and pretend to fiddle a tune as he danced and sang happy songs for children.

The joyfulness of saints often catches us by surprise. It shouldn't—joy is the second of the "fruits of the Spirit," as recorded in Galatians 6.

12

HAVING EYES TO SEE

J. Wesley Ingles was a professor of English literature at Eastern University, a school that has one of the most beautiful campuses of any university anywhere in America.

One day, following a chapel service, Dr. Ingles walked across campus to teach his class. It was a fall day and the leaves had turned an endless array of colors. The sun was shining so that the water on the three ponds was glistening and shimmering with light. Birds were singing and a gentle breeze made the fall day ever so pleasant.

Arriving in class, Dr. Ingles proceeded to describe in rapturous tones the beauty that he had taken in as he walked across campus. He shared, in his poetic way, how all the things he had felt and seen had touched his heart and mind and soul. When he finished, one student, who said he had walked just two steps behind our professor on his way to class, commented, "I think you are getting carried away, Dr. Ingles. It was a lovely day, to be sure, but I was with you and I didn't see all those wonderful things that you describe so eloquently."

Dr. Ingles replied simply, "But don't you wish you could?"

Romans 8:11 tells us that God's Spirit dwelling in us makes us fully alive. That means that we are awakened by His Spirit to the glorious wonders that surround us, but which might otherwise go unnoticed.

13

GRACE RATHER THAN LAW

I was just 21 years old when I became the pastor of the Chesterfield Baptist Church in Chesterfield, New Jersey. I was so young and so excited about the opportunity that when the pulpit committee interviewed me, I didn't ask enough questions or learn all the things about the church that I should have.

I was still in seminary when I took that pastorate and I used to serve the congregation with all the time and energy that I could muster every weekend and at least one day during the week. It was an hour-and-a-half commute, back and forth, from the church to the seminary, so I couldn't be there all the time.

One day the professor who taught the course that I was taking in pastoral care told our class that, the following week, we were each to bring a copy of the constitution of the church where we were serving or attending. We were Baptists and every Baptist church develops its own constitution and bylaws. Our professor wanted us to see that, because Baptists believe in the autonomy of the local church, the constitutions would be very different from each other.

The following weekend, I asked George Longstreet, the elderly farmer who was chairman of the deacons, where I could locate a copy of the church constitution. I realized that I had never seen one. I told George I needed to have a copy of the church constitution for my class.

"You know, there might be a copy of a church constitution around here somewhere," George answered. "I think we might be able to find one for you. Give me a few days and by Wednesday night when you come for prayer meeting, I think I can have one for you."

Surprised by his answer, I asked, "You mean you don't have a church constitution right at hand? How do you run this church if you don't have a constitution or bylaws? How do you do things according to *Robert's Rules of Order*?"

"Bylaws, constitutions, rules of order—Tony, they are for people who don't trust each other. In this little church, we trust each other."

I thought for a moment, and then I said, "George, don't bother getting me a copy of the church constitution. I want to go back and tell the class what you just told me. I wish more churches lived by grace rather than by law."

The fellowship of believers is marked by people who trust each other. Trust is a way of life for those who have entered into a Spirit-filled existence.

14

GRACE FOR OUR ENEMIES

Once a year, in Northern Ireland, there was an event that, from my point of view, seemed to be very spiteful. Protestants who called themselves the Orangemen would march through the Catholic community. Led by a band, they would "stick it" to the Catholics, reminding them how they had been conquered by the army of a Protestant prince and made subject to Protestant overlords. The march always stirred up incredible anger among the Catholics of Portadown, the small city where one of the more offensive marches took place. It was on the eve of one of the marches that I was asked to speak at a peace rally in the Portadown Town Hall.

Preceding me on the program was a Catholic bishop who told a most remarkable story. His mother had come to Northern Ireland from Russia following World War II. The bishop explained that because 40 million Russians had died in that war, almost every family in the environs of Moscow had been directly affected.

When the war was over, the Nazi prisoners of war were taken from their stockade and marched down the main street of Moscow to the train station to be shipped back to Germany. The bishop told how the people of Moscow wanted to get at these prisoners who had brought such devastation and death into their lives. They wanted to tear these Nazis to pieces. The Russian soldiers could barely hold back the angry crowd along the route to the train.

The first group of Nazis who came down the street was the officers—their heads high, their uniforms carefully buttoned, as they marched with typical Nazi arrogance. They were out to demonstrate to the angry mob that they had not been daunted by their imprisonment and were still men of dignity. As the Nazi officers marched toward the train station, the people screamed and yelled obscenities at them, trying to break through the barriers to attack the prisoners.

Then, said the bishop, the crowd suddenly went silent as there came behind the officers the enlisted men. Not having been as well treated as their superiors, they were on the verge of death by starvation. Their bodies were skin and bones. What had been their uniforms were now rags. They were doing their best to make their way toward the train station, the stronger ones holding up the weaker. They were an incredibly wretched sight to behold. The crowd grew silent and then, somehow, a woman broke through the line of Russian soldiers, went up to one of the prisoners, and gave him a piece of bread. Other women ran to their homes and got what little food they could, returning to give what they had to feed the starving enemy soldiers.

"Suddenly those German soldiers were transformed in the eyes of the Russian onlookers that afternoon. No longer were they seen as arrogant, evil men," explained the bishop. "Instead, my mother told me, each of them had become, in the eyes of most of the onlookers, somebody else's little boy, hungry, perhaps dying, and very far away from home."

"And tomorrow," said the bishop to the Catholics assembled at the rally, "as the Orangemen march through your neighborhood, taunting you and saying evil things against you, do your best to look at them and say to yourself, 'Each of them is somebody else's little boy, hungry and dying, and very far away from home.'"

Figuratively speaking, who could argue with that? To be Christian is to view others with a Christlike understanding and empathy.

15

PASS ON THE KINDNESS

As a boy, newly arrived in the United Stated from Italy, my father would spend summer evenings gleaning beans at a farm just outside of Philadelphia. Farmers let him and others glean the beans that had not been picked by the regular pickers, and sell them at a roadside stand. It was a way of making a few extra dollars in the course of a week.

It was hard work, but my father was determined to make the few dollars that would enable him to get a decent place to live and buy food. One evening, when he was picking beans, he looked up from his work and saw, down at the end of a long row, a gigantic African-American man moving quickly, picking beans on either side of the row. He was picking so fast and so effectively that my father knew that it would be no time at all before all the beans that could be picked would be gone.

Exhausted and discouraged, my father simply sat down on the ground with his empty pail between his legs and watched the giant of a man moving toward him. Then, surprisingly, the black man stopped just a few feet in front of my father, smiled, took his bucket of beans and dumped them into my father's bucket. Then, still smiling, he said, "Someday when you see someone who is tired and needs some help, remember what I did for you and you do it for him."

My father never got caught up in the racism that pervaded America in the 1930s and '40s because whenever he met an African-American person, he would think of that giant of a man who had been generous to him in his hour of need. He always told me as I was growing up to forget race because there was goodness and evil in all races, and he had seen the best and the worst in each of them. Lovingkindness is a trait that all Christians should exhibit. When it is lived out, it can break down the barriers that divide people and can make them one.

16

THE COST OF
THE CROSS

Clarence Jordan, preacher and social activist, was once taken on a tour of one of the greatest churches in America. As the tour guide brought him to the very front of the church where he could look up at the altar, he was told by the tour guide: "Do you see that cross? It's a gold cross. It was donated by one of our wealthiest members in memory of his wife. That cross, Mr. Jordan, which is covered with gold leaf, cost over $750,000."

Clarence responded, "Shucks! Time was you could get one for free!"

Christians are people who understand that the call of Christ is a call to sacrifice to meet the needs of others and, in meeting those needs, to willingly abandon conspicuous displays of wealth that waste God's money.

17

TAKING A COMEDIAN
SERIOUSLY

Lenny Bruce, the comedian who committed suicide a year after being put in jail for obscenity, once said, "I know in my heart, by pure
logic, that any man who claims to be a leader of a church is a hus-
tler if he has two suits in a world in which most people have none."
I have never quite known how to respond to his words, given what
Jesus says in the Sermon on the Mount. I know that if we accept
what Jesus said at face value, then there will be radical changes in
our lifestyles.

18

PRIDEFUL PREACHING

When I was in seminary, I had to take a course in homiletics. Each of the students had to prepare and deliver a sermon to the rest of the class. When it came my turn, I was ready. I thought I had a masterpiece on my hands. I had gone through Bible commentaries and made sure I had profound insights from Scripture to declare from the pulpit. I had the sermon perfectly outlined with three points and good illustrations to support every one of them. I had no doubt that I was going to get an A for that sermon. When the class was over, each of the students handed in an evaluation sheet, as did the professor. I will never forget what he wrote across my paper. "A+—A great sermon, but one thing you should remember, Tony. You can't convince people that you are wonderful and that Jesus is wonderful in the same sermon."

In Philippians 2:3, we are told that we should do nothing for "vain glory" (*KJV*). The Spirit-filled Christian has a humble spirit that avoids any semblance of showing off.

19

WHEN SELF GETS IN THE WAY

A woman told me that she was visiting a church in a Midwestern city and after the service some friendly people gathered around to welcome and visit with her. While they were talking, the preacher's 10-year-old son ran up into the pulpit and, with the microphone still on, shouted out to the remaining people, "Look, everybody, I'm in the pulpit!"

One of the congregants turned to the visiting woman and said, cynically, "His father says that every Sunday morning."

In 1 Corinthians 13, we read that a Christian is never "puffed up" (v. 4, *KJV*) and never shows off.

20

GODLY COURTESY

Former South African bishop Desmond Tutu, winner of the Nobel Prize, once related this story when asked how he decided to become an Anglican priest.

One day, he and his mother were walking down the street when a tall, dignified white man, wearing a clerical collar came toward them. In those days of apartheid, it was the custom for black people to step off the sidewalk when a white person approached, and to then lower their heads in respect as the white person passed. However, this time, before young Desmond and his mother could step off the sidewalk, the white man with the clerical collar stepped off the sidewalk, and as the boy and his mother passed by, tipped his hat as a sign of respect, and then went on his way.

Tutu then told how he asked his mother, "Why did that man do that?"

Her answer changed his life. "Because he is an Anglican priest, and the goodness that he has learned from the Scripture has made him into somebody who shows kindness and graciousness, even when it's not expected."

"It was then," said Tutu, "that I decided that I wanted to be an Anglican priest!"

Living out courtesy should be a must in the life of every Christian, and it can have far-reaching effects.

21

DIFFERENT AGENDAS, SHARED COMPASSION

At Eastern University, there is at graduation the opportunity for a student to give an address to share appreciation for all that had been done to make this student's education possible.

One year, a very bright young woman had this honor and, as she mounted the rostrum, there was great expectation that her words would give affirmation to many, especially the parents who had sacrificed much for her scholarly pursuits.

As her speech progressed, the crowd became uneasy as she revealed that every time she had gone home to visit, she had found that she and her politically conservative father had moved farther apart in their thinking. Whereas once they had agreed on everything, it had reached a point where, when it came to political and economic issues, they agreed on almost nothing. Every time they talked, she and her father found themselves more and more ideologically estranged. I can still hear her saying, "Dad! There isn't much we agree on these days when it comes to politics, or when it comes to what our government should be doing for the poor and oppressed of the world."

A sense of anger arose in the crowd. Graduation Day was not the time to publicly pick on your father. This was not a time to embarrass and hurt him. Then suddenly, there was a reversal as she said, "But, Dad, all that I think and all that I do with the rest of my life is your fault. You taught me compassion, and all my political beliefs and all of my life commitments are a result of the compassion that you instilled in me from the time I was a child. Though we may not agree to live out compassion in the same ways, here's to you, Dad! Here's to you! Anything worthwhile I do with my life is your fault. You taught me compassion and all else in my life flows from that."

There were few in the audience without tears in their eyes that day, as a daughter and a father who had great ideological differences were, nevertheless, unified in their love for humanity in the name of Christ.

It was clear that the commonality created by their shared compassion would keep them connected forever.

Different Christians may have different political agendas, but their common commitments to live out love and justice in the world should nurture mutual respect.

22

ACTING LIKE CHRISTIANS

There is a story circulating about Charles Spurgeon, who was not only a great preacher, but also sponsored a variety of ministries for needy people throughout the city of London.

An American residing in Oxford heard about what was being done by Spurgeon and the people of his church and wanted to support these good works with a significant financial contribution, even though he himself was not a religious man.

On an arranged day, Spurgeon and two of his deacons went to visit the man and receive his check for the ministries. When they got to the man's house, he invited them into the living room and proceeded to welcome them by offering each of them an opportunity to take one of his favorite cigars. The two deacons drew back in horror and let it be known by their manner that they did not approve of smoking. Spurgeon, on the other hand, selected a cigar, lit it, and, after a deep puff, commented on how good it was.

On the train back to London, the two deacons were indignant and scolded Spurgeon, saying, "How could you? You're a Baptist pastor! How could you possibly take that man's cigar and smoke it? You know how we feel about such things."

To this, Spurgeon answered, "Well—I felt that one of us had to act like a Christian."

23

FOREVER YOUNG

I joined 48 church leaders in staging a demonstration protesting proposed federal budget cuts that would have severely affected the poor. Within our group was a 90-year-old church leader from Washington, DC, who had been active in many social justice movements during the previous 50 years. On numerous occasions, he had been arrested, and he was about to be arrested again.

We all stood together in the rotunda of the Capitol building, singing hymns and, from time to time, reading from the tenth chapter of Isaiah wherein the prophet declares:

> Woe to those who make unjust laws, to those who issue oppressive decrees, to deprive the poor of their rights and withhold justice from the oppressed of my people, making widows their prey and robbing the fatherless. What will you do on the day of reckoning, when disaster comes from afar? To whom will you run for help? Where will you leave your riches (vv. 1-3, *NIV*)?

Following our arrests, we were at police headquarters being fingerprinted, when the officer behind the desk looked up and, seeing my elderly friend, said, "Are you back here again? When are you going to grow up and stop this foolishness?"

This senior spokesman for the cause of the Kingdom replied, in a strong, clear voice, and with a smile on his face, "When you are filled with God's Spirit and working for justice for the poor, you are forever young!"

Being sure of who you are, and being sure that what you are doing is in accordance with God's will, can make a person "forever young."

24

LOST IN CONSTRUCTION

The details of the history of the Taj Mahal lie shrouded in mystery, lost in antiquity, but among the things we do know about it is that it was constructed by a ruler who, brokenhearted over the death of his wife, wanted to construct a memorial to glorify her. To that end, he hired the best architectural designers he could find. No expense was spared when purchasing building materials. Daily, the bereaved ruler consulted with the architect to be sure that the building would be as beautiful as possible. The symmetry of the building was particularly important to him. He wanted everything to be in perfect balance, and in the exact center of the building he wanted the sarcophagus containing the remains of his dear wife.

They discussed, day in and day out, how to make the building more and more beautiful. Then, one day, the architect finally broached a subject that he had been reluctant to bring up. He pointed out that all that marred the perfect balance of the building was the casket sitting in the middle of the floor. "If that could just be removed," he said, "and placed somewhere else, the building would be a perfect and fitting memorial to your deceased wife."

After thoughtful reflection, and much consultation, the ruler agreed. The casket was removed, and his wife was buried elsewhere. Now, no one is quite sure where she is buried. Her body was lost in the process of building a beautiful edifice in her memory.

Sometimes I think this story is a good metaphor for the church. We have constructed an incredible institution. We have built buildings in the name of Jesus Christ. We have financed elaborate constructions to honor Him. But it may be that, in the midst of all the building and constructing, we have lost sight of Him. In the words of Mary at the tomb, "They have taken away my LORD, and I know not where they have laid Him" (John 10:13, *KJV*).

25

MAKE A JOYFUL NOISE — REALLY!

For 24 years in a row, I was a platform speaker at Creation Festival, a great gathering of young people who come together in central Pennsylvania to hear contemporary Christian bands and listen to speakers with messages especially designed to reach young people. Annually, Creation draws anywhere from 30 to 50 thousand young people, along with their adult sponsors and chaperones.

This Christian festival ends on Saturday night, and one particular year I was the preacher who closed out the program. The next morning, I had been scheduled to preach at a nearby Lutheran church. Word got around at Creation as to where I would be preaching, and many of the young people on their way home stopped by there to participate in the worship. So, instead of the usual 200 or 300 folks in the congregation, that Lutheran Church was packed with about 1,200 people. They filled the downstairs and the balcony, and there were young people standing along both sides of the church.

The Lutheran pastor had no idea how these young people happened to be there, as he remarked to me, "We really advertised your coming widely throughout the area." Little did he know that the young people filling his church were very much of a charismatic bent. Many of them were from Assembly of God churches.

The service began with the pastor, clothed in his robes, standing at the pulpit, in a very formal setting. With lighted candles and all the accessories that go with "high church" worship, he initiated the service by saying in a droning voice, "This is the day that the Lord has made. Let us rejoice and be glad in it. Let us come into His gates with thanksgiving and into His courts with praise."

A young man in the balcony raised his arms and shouted at the top of his lungs, "*All ri-i-i-i-ght!*"

All over the place, young people began to clap and cheer.

I watched as the amazed pastor struggled to comprehend the reaction his words had elicited. He was stunned. The last thing in the world he expected when he called upon the congregation to make a joyful noise unto the Lord was that anybody would.

PART 3

INTIMACY WITH GOD

PART 3

INTIMACY WITH GOD

For you did not receive a spirit of slavery to fall back into fear, but you have received a spirit of adoption. When we cry, "Abba! Father!" it is that very Spirit bearing witness with our spirit that we are children of God, and if children, then heirs, heirs of God and joint heirs with Christ—if, in fact, we suffer with him so that we may also be glorified with him.
ROMANS 8:15-17

We Christians should be able to call God "Abba." This is a name that, for the ancient Jews, suggested an intense intimacy. In these verses, we read that in surrendering ourselves to Christ, and in praying for the Holy Spirit to saturate our lives, we can call God "Abba." We can experience the kind of mystical connectedness with God that can satisfy the deepest longings of our hearts. As we grow into an ever-deepening relationship with God, we learn something of God's character. God will not be some kind of a transcendental potentate, but instead, will be experienced as a loving parent.

I

IS THIS THE SAME GOD?

There was a mission program in the slums of inner-city Philadelphia, to which homeless men came regularly for a free meal and a place to sleep. All that was expected of the men, in return, was that they sit through a sermon.

One evening, the youth group from our church was invited to lead the evening service and the group voted for me to do the preaching. As a young 18-year-old kid, I stood in the pulpit and gave these men a forceful message that had all the markings of a "hellfire and brimstone" tirade. I preached against sin and told the men that they were hellbound if they didn't heed my message and come down the aisle and surrender their lives for conversion.

One of the things about people who have lost everything, including their pride, is that they do not hesitate to say what they really think. Having nothing to lose, they can be right up front about what they are thinking. One of the men shouted out, in the midst of my sermon, "Are you talking about the same God that we heard about last week when an old man was here preaching to us? *He* told us that God was full of love and wanted to help us in spite of all that we may have done, and that God loved us no matter what kind of people we were. It doesn't sound like you're talking about the same God. Your God is angry and condemning. Are you talking about the same God we heard about last week?"

I was taken aback and embarrassed by the man's question. At that point, I remembered that Jesus had come into the world, not to condemn the world, but to reveal God's love. John 3:16-17 makes that very clear.

2

GOD IS NOT THE AUTHOR OF EVIL

With great sadness, the great preacher William Sloan Coffin, who was once dean of the chapel at Yale University, went to the funeral of his son who had been killed in a climbing accident. The minister conducting the service said to the assembled congregation, "We must accept what has happened to this young man as the will of God."

At that, William Sloan Coffin stood and shouted, "The hell it was God's will! When my son died, God was the first one who cried!"

Was he right? Are tragedies the will of God, or are they simply manifestations of what has gone wrong in this world? Are not tragedies what God sent His Son into the world to undo? God loves us too much to will suffering into our lives. The Bible says that God is not willing that any should perish (see 2 Pet. 3:9).

3

GIVING YOURSELF
TO JESUS

Will Campbell, a preacher who calls himself an "apostle to the red-necks," says that he sometimes imagines an evangelist ending a sermon with an invitation for people to have a personal relationship with Christ by saying, "The time has come to give your life to Jesus. Will you do it now? Will you give your life to Jesus right now?"

Responding to the invitation, people begin to get out of their seats and come down the aisle. At that point, the preacher says, "I didn't say to give your life to me; I said to give your life to Jesus. Go and give your life to Jesus."

The people who were coming down the aisle then turn around and leave the church, as the preacher then says to the rest of the congregation, "What about the rest of you? Are you willing to give your lives to Jesus? Are you willing to give your lives to Jesus right now?"

The people stand and move quickly out of the church building, get into their cars and drive away.

Not long afterward, the telephones start ringing off their hooks at the police station. The first caller says, "Officer, get some cops down here to the old folks' home. There are people banging at the door saying, 'We want to meet with Jesus. We want to give ourselves to Jesus.' I keep telling them that Jesus isn't here. The only people here are some forgotten elderly folks waiting to die. Most of them are decrepit. Some are suffering from Alzheimer's. Jesus isn't here, just a bunch of old folks. But these people outside keep yelling, 'Let us in. We want to see Jesus. We want to give ourselves to Jesus.'"

Another call is from the warden down at the local prison, demanding help. "Get some of your troops down here," he barks to the police captain at the station. "There's a bunch of crazies outside, banging on the prison doors and yelling, 'We want to see Jesus.

We want to meet Jesus. We want to give ourselves to Jesus.' I keep telling them Jesus isn't here. The only people here are rapists and murderers and thieves, but it doesn't stop them. They keep yelling, 'We want you to let us in so that we can give ourselves to Jesus.'"

Another caller asks that something be done about the weird people gathered outside the AIDS hospice, demanding to see Jesus, asking for the opportunity to give themselves to Jesus. The caller explains that he has told the crowd that the only people they have in this place are some folks suffering from AIDS. "I told these crazies that some of our patients are sexual perverts, and that all of them are near death, but it doesn't seem to deter them. They keep saying, 'Oh, no. We know that Jesus is in there, waiting to be embraced and loved, and we have come to give ourselves to Jesus.'"

Will concludes by saying, "I could almost hear Jesus Himself saying to me, 'Whatever you do for one of the least of these, you do for Me.'"

Entering into intimacy with God will always lead to intimacy with those who are needy and oppressed. It is the nature of God to come to us through those who suffer, and to reach through us to those who are in need.

4

BEING ALONE WITH JESUS

As a teenager, I hated going to Sunday evening church. It wasn't that I was down on church; it was just that on Sunday evenings the preacher was never prepared. In the morning the sermon had three points and a poem and then you were out of there, but in the evening, the preacher was all over the place. You knew he was just shooting from the hip. Worse than that, he hadn't even picked out the hymns. You can always tell when the preacher hasn't picked out the hymns because he looks over the congregation with a big smile as though he's doing the people a favor and says, "Tonight I'm going to let you pick the hymns. Does anybody have a favorite?"

On most Sunday evenings at my church back then, Mrs. Kirkpatrick, who always sat on the right-hand side, three rows back, would raise her hand and say, "One-twenty-two in the Tabernacle hymnal!"

I hated 122 in the Tabernacle hymnal because I was a kid who had learned to survive on the tough streets of West Philadelphia by acting tough. I never got into a fight because I didn't have to fight. I knew how to walk. I knew how to saunter down the street with an insolent look on my face and stare people down. Nobody messed with me. I wasn't really all that tough, but projecting a tough image was my protection.

On Sunday evenings I would saunter into church and sit down next to my mother who insisted that I be there for every service. Slouched in my seat, I would cringe inwardly when we had to sing 122 in the Tabernacle hymnal. It just was *not* the kind of song that a kid who's trying to act tough wants to sing:

"I come to the garden alone, while the dew is still on the roses . . ."

To me, at age 15, that song seemed awfully "icky," and the second verse was even worse:

"He speaks and the sound of His voice is so *sweet* the birds hush their singing . . ."

That hymn definitely did not fit my macho image, and I hated it. But that's because I was 15. The older I get, the more I love to sing 122 in the Tabernacle hymnal. The older I get, the more I love to sing:

"And He walks with me and He talks with me, and He tells me I am His own; and the joy we share, as we tarry there, none other has ever known."

You've got to get some years under your belt before you can feel yourself wrapped in those words and enjoy the spiritual fulfillment of "going to the garden" alone, where, especially in the stillness of the night, you can feel His presence permeate your being and saturate your soul.

5

ADOPTION WITH NO STRINGS ATTACHED

A young couple, having discovered that they would not be able to have children, decided to adopt an older child. They contacted a Christian adoption agency, and then proceeded to fill out the papers and go through the interviews necessary for adopting a child. One day the good news came that there was a 10-year-old boy who needed a home and was available to this couple. They were overjoyed.

The couple proceeded to prepare a bedroom just for him. They put up wallpaper that had footballs, basketballs, and baseballs on it. They got him a very special bed, and filled the room with toys that a young boy would love.

When the day for the adoption came, the couple went to meet with the social worker who presented them with their new son. They brought him home and took him up to see his new bedroom. The boy was overawed by all he saw. The sports equipment, the toys, the bed, the wallpaper—all were beyond his wildest imagination. But the new parents noticed something; the boy did not seem to be very happy with it all. As a matter of fact, they began to sense some negative vibes. Puzzled, they asked their newly adopted son if there was anything wrong.

The boy answered, "You're giving me all of this, and you say that this is my bedroom. You tell me I get to live here and that all of this is mine to keep. What I want to know is, what do I have to do to get this stuff? What do you expect from me in order for me to keep this stuff and have this great room?"

The parents, somewhat taken aback by the boy's questions, simply answered, "You don't have to do anything. All we want is for you to love us. We already love you, and we want you to love us back. That's it. There's nothing more to it than that. All of this is yours simply because we love you and want you to love us in return."

So it is with the salvation story. God has given us salvation as a gift. We don't have to earn it. We don't have to prove that we deserve it. All God wants is our love.

6

THINGS VERSUS INTIMACY

Richard Rohr, the Franciscan social activist and preacher, tells about a prayer he heard following one of his sermons when he was preaching in Africa. An old man prayed, "Lord, let us never move into stone houses." Rohr had no idea what the prayer meant. Afterward, when he inquired of the old man why he had prayed the way he did, the old man said, "You know Africa. You have seen our country. People here live in huts, and the huts have no doors. That is why your family is my family, and my family is your family. But as soon as you move into a stone house, you build a door. On the door you put a lock, and behind your door you begin to accumulate more and more things. Then you have to spend the rest of your life protecting all that you have acquired."

That story reminded me of those people who become so consumed with the cares of this world that they forget what is really important—intimacy with others, which in turn, can be intimacy with God.

7

TRIVIAL PURSUITS

There's a game called Trivial Pursuit. I find the title of the game most interesting because so many of us do spend good chunks of our lives in trivial pursuits. I recently read of a man who spent five years of his life constructing a model of the Empire State Building out of toothpicks. This is hardly a way of "redeeming the time," as the Bible says.

The greatest thing we can do, according to Jesus, is to love God with heart, soul and mind. Such intimacy with God is demonstrated by loving our neighbors as ourselves. Relaxing by enjoying a hobby is a good thing, unless it keeps us from the ultimate pursuit that is spelled out in what is called "The Greatest Commandment" (Matt. 22:36-40, *NIV*).

8

THE WONDER OF THE ORDINARY

One day, while confined to bed with a stomach virus, I found myself surfing the television channels. For some unknown reason, I settled on watching *Mister Rogers' Neighborhood*, a show for children on the Public Broadcasting Service. Before I even realized what was happening, I found myself caught up in what this friendly, gentle man was saying, listening intently as he explained, "Boys and girls, I am going to fill this fish tank with water. The fish need to have clean water, and I am going to give them some clean water right now. Watch me carefully." I was captivated by what Mister Rogers was doing. He took a glass, filled it with water, and poured it into the glass fish tank. And then, slowly, he poured another glass of water, and then another, and another. With each glass, he made some comment about how wonderful it was to be able to give the fish a gift as wonderful as clean water.

Without realizing it, I was carried back to my childhood and, as Mister Rogers poured each glass of water into the fish tank, I felt a sense of awe. At one point, I actually whispered, "Wow!" Then I caught myself, and became a grownup again. That was a shame. *Children* have the capacity to experience the wonder of ordinary events and common things.

I believe that, when we are alive in the Spirit of God, our sense of childlike wonder can be restored and we can become as little children.

In the end, spirituality always brings with it a sense of the wonder of what is too often unnoticed or dismissed as ordinary.

PART 4

THE CALL TO
RESCUE CREATION

PART 4

THE CALL TO
RESCUE CREATION

*I consider that the sufferings of this present time are not worth
comparing with the glory about to be revealed to us. For the creation
waits with eager longing for the revealing of the children of God; for the
creation was subjected to futility, not of its own will but by the will of the
one who subjected it, in hope that the creation itself will be set free
from its bondage to decay and will obtain the freedom of the glory of the
children of God. We know that the whole creation has been groaning in
labor pains until now; and not only the creation, but we ourselves, who
have the first fruits of the Spirit, groan inwardly while we wait for
adoption, the redemption of our bodies.*
ROMANS 8:18-23

Intimacy with God inevitably leads to our hearts being broken by
the things that break the heart of God. As God permeates our being, the concerns of God become our concerns. Consequently, we
are driven into the world, as was God's Son, to address the sufferings of the world.

All of creation is in a fallen condition. Evil forces have moved
throughout the world causing havoc. Racism, sexism, poverty, homophobia, violence, environmental degradation, cruelty, injustice
and disease seem evident everywhere. In these verses, we are told
that creation waits for God-infused Christians to rescue it from
these painful realities.

I

WHEN BORN AGAIN DOESN'T DO IT

Several years ago, a very prominent evangelist prepared to go to the city of Jackson, Mississippi, to conduct a series of evangelistic meetings. Prior to the meetings, he called together the pastors and preachers of the city to give them an overview of the way in which his messages would unfold. He shared with them the themes of his messages and explained what he expected them to do as partners in the effort to spread the gospel throughout their community.

When the evangelist ended his presentation and asked for questions, an old African-American preacher rose and, in a halting, stumbling fashion, slowly asked, "Preacher? Just what do you hope to accomplish in this town anyway? What do you hope is going to happen here? Can you tell us that?"

The evangelist quickly shot back, "I want to see every citizen of Jackson, Mississippi, become a born-again Christian!"

To that, the old black preacher answered, "Mister! Ever since I was a little boy, there have been people who have treated me like dirt—folks who made me feel like less than nothing when they cheated me and talked to me like I was nobody. And you know what? Most of these folks called themselves born-again Christians. And now you're telling me you want everybody in Jackson to be like them?"

That old preacher raised the issue of what it actually means to be born-again, and whether or not people who have had born-again experiences really have been changed by Jesus. Saved people are constrained by God's love to enter the struggle to end the oppression of racism.

2

RESCUING THE SOUL
OF A NATION

Mark Hatfield, the one-time senator from Oregon, was heard to have said, "Christianity was born in Israel. They took it to Greece and made it into a philosophy. They took it to Rome and made it into an institution. They took it to the rest of Europe and made it into a culture. Then they brought it to America, where they made it into a business enterprise." Who can deny the truth of that most interesting and profound statement?

When Hitler came to power, he recognized that it was necessary to pacify the church lest it become a countervailing power to his totalitarian goals. In order to pacify the church, he called pastors together to explain to them the good that he had in mind for Germany. The young Dietrich Bonhoeffer, who was among the pastors gathered for this occasion, listened as Adolf Hitler explained that he would in no way interfere with their ministry to the needy souls of Germany. Bonhoeffer followed Hitler's presentation with a simple statement: "I am concerned about the souls of the people, but I am also concerned about the soul of the nation. What will happen to the soul of the nation in the days that lie ahead?"

As Hitler stomped out of the room, he was overheard to remark, "Let these pastors worry about the souls of men. I will take care of the soul of the nation!"

This story illustrates clearly that it is never enough to simply minister to the needs of *individuals*. God has called us not only to win people to Christ, but also to wrestle against the principalities and the powers and the rulers of this age (see Eph. 6:12).

3

REAL
OBSCENITY

The famous sex icon Mae West had one of her striptease shows in New York City closed down because of the intervention of some of the leading clergy of that city. When they confronted her, scolding her for "obscene behavior," she responded, "I'll tell you what's obscene. It's you people who are supposed to be men of God but do not stand up to those politicians who make wars. I'll tell you what's obscene. It's you preachers who live like rich men instead of calling your people and yourselves to give what you have to meet the needs of the poor. I'll tell you what's obscene. It's churches that spend thousands of dollars for stained glass windows and claim that's what Jesus would do with the money."

You have to wonder why a sex icon should have to speak like a prophet sent from God to challenge us to address obscenities that, in our pieties, we often ignore.

4

WASTED RESOURCES AND WASTED TIME

Søren Kierkegaard, the Danish philosopher and theologian of the nineteenth century, made a habit of making so much of what goes on in the name of Christianity seem ludicrous. His analogies for the church are pithy and stinging. One of the best is a story in which he describes a whole host of men running around, setting up and testing a great array of deep-sea diving equipment. Eventually, the diver appears. They dress him in the heavy suit. They test all the pipes that would give him oxygen, and then Kierkegaard drives home his point by saying that when all of this is done, the deep-sea diver climbs into a bathtub and pulls out the plug. It doesn't take much imagination to see this as a metaphor for the fact that the church is a huge apparatus that spends a lot of time and energy on doing things that, in the end, are of little consequence. If only the church used its resources and its time to do the great things of the kingdom of God.

5

A VOICE FOR THE POOR

After graduating from Eastern University with top honors, one of my former students, Bryan Stevenson, went on to study law at Harvard University. To the surprise of many, following his graduation from Harvard, Bryan did not go into a lucrative legal practice where he could easily have earned as much as half a million dollars a year. Instead, this African-American graduate of Harvard Law School went to Montgomery, Alabama, and started a nonprofit organization that provides legal help for prisoners on death row.

On one occasion, I asked Bryan whether he was opposed to the whole idea of capital punishment. To this, he responded, "How can any Christian believe in capital punishment when Jesus said, 'Blessed are the merciful; for they shall obtain mercy' (Matt. 5:7, KJV)? But even if you did believe in capital punishment, how could you support it in a country where there are two kinds of justice: one kind of justice for rich people and another kind of justice for poor people? And if you don't know that's true, you are really detached from reality."

"The poor," Bryan said, "go to the death chamber in this state not just because they are guilty, which may or may not be the case, but because when they have their day in court they have no one really good to stand up and speak for them."

Then he went on, with a smile on his face, "Except in Montgomery, Alabama, because in Montgomery, Alabama, Doc, I speak for the poor. I speak for the poor and, Doc, I'm good. I'm really good."

I thought to myself, *Bryan, you don't know how good you are. You committed yourself to living out a calling from God to be a voice for those who have no voice, and you have been willing to pay the price that went with such a calling.*

6

TOO BUSY TO HELP

In Flaubert's novel, *Madame Bovary*, the tragic woman in the story is tempted to escape the emptiness of her life by having a sexual affair with her gardener. She goes running to the nearby church to ask the priest to pray for her and help her. As she approaches the priest, she cries out, "Father! Father! I've got troubles!"

To this, the priest answers, "Troubles! Troubles! Everybody's got troubles," and walks away. He had too much on his mind that day, and too much to do, to pay any attention to this desperate woman. Madame Bovary leaves the church and goes back to her estate where she enters into the adulterous relationship that destroys her life.

How often, in our busyness, do we neglect urgent needs? We have to ask ourselves if our busyness sometimes keeps us from rescuing the perishing and caring for the dying.

7

STANDING UP FOR JUSTICE

In the film *To Kill a Mockingbird*, Gregory Peck plays the role of a lawyer named Atticus who defends a black man falsely accused of trying to rape a white woman in a southern town. The case has electrified the community and the courtroom is packed as Atticus does his best to show conclusively that there was no way that the man accused could have committed the crime.

Most of the town's white people are squeezed into the main floor of the courtroom, and in the balcony, huddled together, are the black citizens of the community. Among them sits Atticus's daughter, Scout.

After Atticus has done his best to no avail, the courtroom empties except for the black citizens and Scout, who are still sitting in the balcony.

Unaware of who is in the balcony, Atticus packs his papers in his briefcase and slowly walks toward the door at the back of the courtroom. The black citizens rise to their feet to honor the man who has stood for justice in the face of white racism.

Scout is still trying to figure out what is going on when the black preacher next to her reaches down, grabs her arm, and tells her to stand.

"Get up!" he says, "Your father is passing by."

There are heroes in this world who deserve our respect because they dare to stand for the truth of God in spite of what the cost might be, undeterred by the persecution they will have to endure.

8

SALVATION FOR ANIMALS

There is a story taken from the *Acts of Philip*, one of the five principal apostolic romances written at the end of the fourth century, that tells of how Philip, along with Bartholomew and Miriam, under the leading of the Lord, traveled to the land of Ophiani. As they traveled through a forest, there suddenly came upon them a great leopard who cast himself at Philip's feet and spoke with a human voice. The leopard said, "Hear me, Philip, groomsman of the divine Word, last night I passed through a flock of goats and I seized a kid. When I went into the woods to eat it, after I had wounded it, it took on a human voice and wept like a child, saying, 'Oh, leopard, put off your fierce heart and the beastlike part of your nature, and put on mildness, for an apostle of God is about to pass through this place.'"

At these words, the leopard confessed that he was perplexed and he did not eat the kid. Then he explained that, as he lifted up his eyes, he saw Philip and his friends coming and he knew that they were the servants of God. With this recognition, the leopard ran to Philip and his companions and begged them, "Put off my beastlike nature."

Philip asked the leopard to take him to where the wounded kid could be found; and when they got to that place, Philip prayed over the lamb, "Now know we a truth, that there is none that surpasses Your compassion, oh Jesus, lover of man; for you protect us and convince us by these creatures to believe more and earnestly fulfill our trust. Now, therefore, Lord Jesus Christ, come and grant life and breath and secure existence to these creatures, that they may forsake their beastly nature and come entertain us and no longer eat flesh. And may men's hearts be given to them so that they may be our friends to Your glory."

Reading those words, one cannot help hearkening back to Romans 8:22-23, which reminds us that all of creation is groaning and suffering in pain, and that not only did our Savior come into the world to save us, but that all the creatures of God's creation are waiting for us to deliver them from the bondage of their suffering.

9

POLITICS AS LOVE IN ACTION

We are all aware of the parable of the good Samaritan in which Jesus tells about the man who fell among thieves on the road to Jericho, and how a Samaritan rescued him, took him to an inn, and then provided money for his care and sustenance. But suppose the story had continued. Suppose the good Samaritan had formed a committee called "The Committee for Making the Jericho Road Safe." Suppose the committee had conducted marches, raised public awareness, and forced city hall to put decent lighting along the Jericho road, remove the bushes in which thieves could hide, and make sure that there would be policemen to patrol that highway? Would this not also be a way to express love? And if the city hall, policemen and politicians had been found to be accepting bribes in return for not interfering with the robbers, would it not also be an act of love to organize people to vote the corrupt politicians out of office at the next election? Doesn't God call us to set things right?

IO

WHAT TO DO UNTIL HE RETURNS

Sometimes when I am preaching, I like to call attention to the fact that nobody knows when Jesus will return. Those would-be prophets who seem to have figured it all out and actually announce dates when Christ will return are obviously off the wall. I tell my listeners that I am not embarrassed about not knowing when Christ will come back because Jesus Himself did not know when He would return and set up His kingdom here on earth. Jesus explained to His disciples that the Son of man did not know, the angels did not know, and that if they wanted to know the exact time of His return, they would have to ask Hal Lindsey or some American evangelist! I always get a laugh when I say that.

No one knows the day or the hour of Christ's return, but this we do know: until then, we are called to win the lost and to try to change the world into the world that ought to be. The Bible tells us that the God who begins to do such things in us and through us will complete this good work on the day of His coming (see Phil. 1:6).

II

FRUITS OF REVIVAL

J. Edwin Orr, the one-time professor of missions and church history at Fuller Theological Seminary, became an expert in the study of the great Welsh revival of 1906. Seldom has a revival swept over a nation as that revival swept over the people of Wales. People's lives were radically changed.

Along the southern seacoast of Wales, stretching from Swansea to Cardiff, were several shipyards. For many years, the men who worked in those shipyards had pilfered tools—items ranging from hammers to wheelbarrows. When the revival struck, these men felt that true repentance required that they return what they had stolen. So many of them brought back stolen goods that the shipyards were soon overwhelmed. Orr loved to tell people that he had records indicating that, at some of the shipyards, signs were put up that read something like this: "If you have been converted because of the recent revival and are planning to return things that you have stolen from this shipyard, please do not do so. Keep what you have stolen. We have no more room for stolen goods."

Such are the fruits of revival! It always results in changing what goes on in the world.

12

CHANGED INDIVIDUALS CHANGE SOCIETY

When I became a social activist, some of my evangelical friends told me that this was a waste of time. I can remember many of them saying, "Don't you realize that all our attention should be given to winning people to Christ? Christ can change their lives and it is changed individuals who change society." I thought about that for a long time. Through Christ, I had become a changed individual who wanted to change society, but the very persons who told me that changed individuals change society now opposed my attempts to change society.

13

LIVING THE LIFE IS NOT ENOUGH

Every once in a while, I meet someone who says something like, "I don't think you have to go around telling people about Jesus. I think all you have to do is live the life that Jesus wants you to live so others can see that life and want to become Christians themselves. That's what I do."

What arrogance! Stop to think about it. These persons are saying, "I don't have to explain Jesus to anybody. I am so righteous that all I have to do is let people take a good look at me and they will fall over converted."

I don't know about you, but there are enough flaws and shortcomings in my life for me not to want people to look too closely lest they be disillusioned in a big way. I don't preach myself; I preach Christ. I do not hold myself up; I hold Him up. I have to tell people about Jesus because only He embodies the goodness that is worthy of emulation. All the rest of us fall short of the glory of God. It is through hearing the gospel story that others gain the opportunity to enter into a transforming relationship with God—and transformed people are the instruments of love and justice who can transform the world (see Rom. 10:15).

14

ALL THEY EVER
TALK ABOUT

My friend and one-time co-author William Willimon, a Methodist preacher and bishop, was once told by his six-year-old son what many fathers have heard on Sunday mornings. "I don't want to go to church," said young Willimon.

When Will asked why, the boy answered, "Because church is boring!"

"Why do you think it's boring?" asked the preacher father.

"Well, all they ever talk about there is Jesus," answered the son. "Jesus, Jesus, Jesus, Jesus, Jesus. That's all you hear in that place. All you hear is people talking about Jesus."

If only that were true about every church! Talking about Jesus is essential if the world is to be saved.

15

GETTING THE BIG PICTURE

One year our mission work in Camden, New Jersey, scheduled a neighborhood cleanup day. We gave the boys and girls big plastic bags and told them to spread out through the neighborhood and pick up all kinds of trash, along with broken bottles and discarded beer cans. With great enthusiasm, the children followed the instructions to work to make their neighborhood a better place to live.

I happened to be driving through the neighborhood that day when I saw a small boy, who couldn't have been more than eight years old, pulling a huge plastic bag filled with trash. I leaned out the car window and yelled, "Hey, kid, what are you doing?" The boy, who did not know me, called back, "Hey, mister, *I'm cleaning up America!*"

Sometimes what the good God calls us to do may seem small, but if we can see it as part of something much bigger, we will be empowered to keep working to build the kingdom of God on earth as it is in heaven.

16

FATHER ZOSSIMA'S ADVICE

In Dostoevsky's famous novel, *The Brothers Karamazov*, the priest, whose values dominate the story, tells the brothers, "Love all God's creation, the whole of it, and every grain of sand. Love every leaf, every ray of God's light! Love the animals. Love the plants. Love everything, and if you love everything you will perceive the divine mystery in things."

17

DOING WHAT THEY HAD TO DO

A friend of mine told me about visiting a village in Malawi that had been devastated by AIDS. He couldn't find anyone there who was over the age of 18. All the older men and women had died. Almost every morning, coming into the village would be 8 to 12 taxicabs, and the drivers would shout out to the teenage women steeped in poverty, "Come work with us for the day. You have brothers and sisters to feed. You have no jobs. You have no way to make money. Come work with us. At the end of the day, we will share the money and you will be able to buy food for your brothers and sisters."

We all know what kind of work these taxicab drivers had for these young women, and no doubt you find that "work" as disgusting as I do. However, having said that, I would also have to say that there may be something noble about a young woman who is willing to allow some filthy "john" to drool over her naked body in order to get a few dollars to buy food for her hungry brothers and sisters. Such sacrifice cannot easily be condemned.

I often tell that story when I am trying to get people in a congregation to sign up to sponsor a child through World Vision or Compassion International. I do my best to explain that for 32 dollars a month it is possible to clothe, feed, educate and evangelize a child in a Third World country, and perhaps even keep a child from being forced into the degradation of prostitution. While it may not be possible to change the whole world, it *is* possible to change the world for one child.

18

A SHOCKING PRAYER

A preacher I know was on a tour of mission work in Zimbabwe. He visited a clinic that had been overwhelmed by people suffering from AIDS. In the waiting room, which was about the size of a typical classroom, there were more than a hundred women squeezed in, sitting on benches.

My preacher friend was stunned by the dead silence of the women in the room. They sat with bowed heads and downcast eyes, many of them holding crying children on their laps. Not knowing what else to do, he sat down beside one woman and asked if he could pray with her. "Yes!" she responded. "I would like you to pray that my children die before I do."

My friend was shocked by that request, but he did understand why this mother had said what she did. He had seen the children who had been orphaned by the AIDS crisis and left to die on the streets of the city. He realized that what this mother wanted was to be there for her sick children and to care for them in the last hours of their lives here on earth. She wanted to be the one to hold their hands and to pray for them and comfort them as they faced the great unknown. Like her, her children had AIDS and would die. Her prayer was that she live long enough to lovingly embrace her children as they passed into eternity.

When he returned to the clinic two weeks later, that mother told him that God had answered his prayer. Both of her children had died and now she could die in peace, knowing they would not be left on the streets to beg, alone and afraid in their final hours.

19

PULLING DOWN
THE SHADES

I was in Port-au-Prince, Haiti. I had come to the country to check on the mission work that some of the young men and women who serve in our missionary programs in that desperate nation carry out day in and day out. I wanted to see to it that our workers were surviving emotionally and spiritually. At the end of a long day of ministry, I was tired and "peopled-out," so it was with great relief that I sat down to eat a good dinner at a French restaurant in the heart of Port-au-Prince. I was seated next to the window so I could enjoy watching the activity on the streets outside.

The waiter brought a delicious-looking meal and set it in front of me. I picked up my knife and fork and was about to dive in when I happened to look to my right. There, with their noses pressed flat against the window, staring at my food, were four ragged street urchins, four of the hundreds and hundreds of hungry, sometimes starving, boys and girls on the streets of the city. With their faces right up against the glass, they were staring at the food on my plate.

The waiter, seeing my discomfort, quickly moved in and pulled down the window shade, shutting out the disturbing sight of the hungry children. Then he said to me, "Don't let them bother you. Enjoy your meal." As if I could!

But isn't that what most of us do? Don't we all have a tendency to "pull down the shade" and shut out the 35,000 children who die every day from either starvation or diseases related to malnutrition? Don't we all want to go on enjoying our meals and pretending that they aren't there? Don't we all try to "pull down the shade" and shut them out of our lives?

In the New Testament, Jesus tells the story of the rich man and Lazarus. He describes a rich man who fares sumptuously every day, dressed in fine clothes, and living in a fine house. At the gates of his estate is a poor man named Lazarus who is covered with sores and who is starving. He would love to have the leftover garbage from the rich man's meal, but no one gives him anything.

Jesus, in telling the story, says that both these men die. Lazarus, the starving beggar at the gates, goes to heaven, which is described as "Abraham's bosom" (*NKJV*). The rich man, on the other hand, goes to a place where he is engulfed by flames.

As I read that story, I thought to myself, "Why did the rich man end up in hell? Had he committed adultery? Had he murdered someone? Had he been a deceiver, a thief? What great sin had he committed to deserve this fate?" Then it dawned on me that he had simply eaten great meals while remaining indifferent to a person who was in desperate need of help. The rich man had lived the good life, all the while pulling down his shade so that he didn't have to see the poor man, Lazarus, who writhed in agony at his very gate.

Let us call upon God to help us raise the shade and make us see those whom we are called to serve with love and sacrifice.

20

WHAT GOES AROUND COMES AROUND

My grandmother was an immigrant from Italy, and it wasn't long after she settled in Philadelphia that my grandfather was killed in a trolley car accident and she was left on her own to raise three children, my mother being the eldest. These were the days before there was any public assistance provided by the government for poor families. It was in the early 1900s and families like my mother's family were left desperately alone and on the verge of starvation.

My grandmother tried to get help, but there seemed to be none available. The Catholic Church she had been attending was overwhelmed with poor people, all of whom were begging for assistance, and the resources of the church were limited. She tried to find an orphanage that would take in my mother and her two brothers, but each of the places where she applied required that both parents be deceased before children could be accepted.

One day, in despair, my grandmother wrote a note and gave it to my mother. She instructed my mother to wait an hour, then take that note to the police station two blocks away and hand it to the policeman. It simply stated that by the time this note was read my grandmother would have committed suicide and that these three children had no father or mother and were therefore eligible for acceptance into the nearby orphanage.

My mother tells of huddling with her two brothers in the cold basement room that they called home, wondering what was happening and why. My grandmother, who had left the children, was wandering in a staggering fashion toward the nearby Delaware River. I could never find out whether she really intended to kill herself or whether she just planned to disappear, but the good news is she didn't have to do either.

Talking out loud as she stumbled down the street, the distraught woman caught the attention of a young seminary student named Everett Griffith. He was working out of a Baptist mission in south Philadelphia and happened to be proficient in learning languages. He had learned the Italian language so that he could minister to the huge population of Italian immigrants that had settled in this part of the city. This young seminarian intercepted my grandmother, calmed her down, and tried to understand why she was so upset. When he heard the story, he acted quickly, telling my grandmother that it was not necessary for her to do anything drastic. He went with her to gather up my mother and her two brothers and took them to his own little apartment to stay until he could find them a better place to live. He got my nine-year-old mother a job cleaning jewelry for a number of jewelry stores on what is called Jewelers' Row in Philadelphia. The money she earned was sufficient for my grandmother to eke out a living for herself and her children. Needless to say, it wasn't long before my grandmother and her children were part of the Baptist mission and worshiping regularly under the leadership of the young, soon-to-be-ordained preacher who had rescued them.

My father and his brother came to America from Sicily following a horrendous earthquake that destroyed his whole family except for his brother and one sister. None of them had any economic means of support. The sister went to a nunnery, figuring that was her only option for survival. My father and his brother scraped together enough money to come to America. Understanding that this was the land of opportunity, they sought help and hope in this new land.

It wasn't long after they arrived in America that my father's older brother died and he was left, at age 15, alone, to fend for himself. He had no grasp of English and his future looked bleak. World War I had broken out, but the United States had not yet joined the war. My father figured that he could survive if he could make his way up to Canada, lie about his age, and join the Canadian army, where at least he would have food to eat. That's what he did, and when he was just 16 years of age, he was on the Western Front where he was victimized by the first attack of mustard gas (which at that time was legal in warfare). He was brought back to Montreal and slowly nursed back to health. In the meantime, his sister had left the nunnery and found the means to get to Philadelphia to look for her brothers, hoping that together they could set up housekeeping. When my father left the hospital, he returned to Philadelphia, met up with his sister, and tried to find employment. Sadly, there were no jobs to be found in Philadelphia at that time, but, through an amazing set of circumstances, my father happened to meet up with the same seminary student who had been so important in rescuing my mother's family. Everett Griffith found my father a job cleaning windows at the Benjamin Franklin Hotel in downtown Philadelphia, and life turned around for my father and for his sister, who, for the first time, had a future that was filled with hope.

Needless to say, it wasn't long before my father was a member of the little Baptist mission pastored by Everett Griffith.

Fast forward to when I was a senior at Eastern University and the president of the school's missionary society. Each year Eastern had what we called "Spiritual Vision Week," during which we brought in an outstanding speaker to challenge young people to make commitments to Christ. One particular year, the speaker was a Hebrew scholar named Dr. Everett Griffith. Neither he nor I were aware of the connections that we had to each other, but as we sat on the platform of the school auditorium, making small talk before the service started, Dr. Griffith asked me my name. When I told him that it was Tony Campolo, he responded by saying that he once knew a Tony Campolo when he was a young man serving in a Baptist mission in south Philadelphia. Without hesitation, I said, "That was my father."

"If that was your father," said Dr. Griffith, "then I was the one who performed the wedding that married him to Mary Piccerelli. I married your parents." Then he looked at me and asked, "What are you planning to do with your life?"

When I told him that I was committed to the Christian ministry, he started to cry and it took him quite a while to compose himself. The idea that his good works of mercy many years earlier had not only rescued some people who were in desperate need, but also had led to a young man going into the gospel ministry, brought him more joy than I can tell you.

Whenever anyone asks me why I so naturally combine traditional evangelism with the social gospel, I always have to answer, "It's a long story, and someday when you have the time I'll tell you about it." Now you know that story.

21

THE NEED FOR LOVE

American psychologist Rene Spitz conducted a study at a South American foundling home where 97 babies, ranging in age from three months to three years, lived. They were adequately fed and cared for medically, but a shortage of nurses robbed these children of the loving attention that most babies get. For most of the day, they were left to themselves. Within three months, abnormalities began to show up. There was a loss of appetite, inability to sleep, and general loss of interest in life. By the end of five months, the deterioration of these children had accelerated. Most of them had shrunken bodies. Emotionally starved, they whimpered and trembled. Their faces twisted in grotesque ways. Twenty-seven of the children died in their first year, and seven more before age two. Of those who survived, 21 were so affected that they were hopeless neurotics for the rest of their lives. Everyone needs love, and we Christians are called to give it.

22

TENDERHEARTED PROPHET

William Sloan Coffin, one-time chaplain at Yale University and pastor of the great Riverside Church in New York City, was a strong antiwar advocate. One Sunday, as he delivered a blistering sermon against militarism, an army colonel in the congregation struggled to restrain himself.

After the service, the colonel confronted Coffin in the receiving line at the back of the church. With an angry edge to his voice, he said, "It was all I could do to stay in my seat. What I wanted to do was to stand up, march out the center aisle, and halfway to the rear of the church, turn and shout at the top of my lungs, 'B***s***!'"

"Why didn't you?" asked his pastor.

"Because the night my wife died, you stayed up all night, sitting at her bedside, holding her hand, and praying with her," was the reply.

A minister can only be a prophet to the people of the congregation if the right to be heard has first been earned by being an intensely loving pastor.

23

CHARITY AND JUSTICE

One year, Bono, the famous rock star, was the featured speaker at the National Prayer Breakfast in Washington, DC. Present were President George W. Bush, most of his Cabinet, an array of senators and members of Congress, along with various ambassadors, and several heads of state. The audience of more than 2,500 persons was composed predominantly of church leaders. When Bono rose to speak, he began by commending the church leaders for their works of charity. He pointed out that, in Africa, and in other places where there is tremendous need, church people have been there, ministering to those who suffer, and bringing along with them vast resources to help meet the needs of the poor and the oppressed. Then, turning to the president, he went on to say, "But I haven't come to talk about charity today; I have come to talk about justice."

Bono went on to declare that there was a desperate need for the US government to do justice for the poor of Africa, and for the poor in the rest of the world. He cited the fact that less than four-tenths of 1 percent of the federal budget had been designated for helping the poor of the world, and pled for that amount to be doubled to 0.8 percent. The rock star went on to make it clear that this would only be the beginning of living out the justice required from a country that has only 6 percent of the world's population but consumes 43 percent of the world's resources.

Certainly America owes more to the needy of the world.

"To whom much has been given, much will be required" (Luke 12:48).

PART 5

LIVING WITH HOPE

PART 5

LIVING WITH HOPE

*For in hope we were saved. Now hope that is seen is not hope.
For who hopes for what is seen? But if we hope for what we do not see,
we wait for it with patience.*
ROMANS 8:24-25

In Hebrews 11:1, we are told that faith is the substance of things hoped for and the evidence of things not seen. To be Christians is to be people filled with hope. We are people, who, even when facts to the contrary fly in our faces, go on believing that the good we pray for will eventually become a reality. We have hope for lost souls. We have hope for healing. We have hope for the kind of world wherein all will be well. Furthermore, our hopes are not limited to what happens in this world. Our hopes have eternal dimensions.

I

THE KING HAS ONE MORE MOVE

I tried hard to confirm this story because I have heard that the person being described was none other than one-time world chess champion Bobby Fischer.

In the story, a chess master, along with a friend, went to see the Ingmar Bergman film *The Seventh Seal*. The plot of this classic film revolves around a medieval knight who engages in a game of chess with death (the evil one). Throughout the film these two make moves on each other. Then, as the movie comes to a climax, the Prince of Darkness makes a move and, with great finality, utters the word "Checkmate!"

With that, the curtain comes down, and the movie is over.

According to the story, the chess master, who was sitting in the audience, turned to his friend and, in a puzzled tone, exclaimed, "Why is he giving up? The king has one more move! The king has one magnificent move left that can turn the tide and win the game."

Now *that* preaches.

To the mother who is worried because her son seems to be hopelessly hooked on drugs, there is hope in the message: The King has one more move!

To the father, on the verge of despair because his daughter is being sucked into a punk rock subculture marked by sexual promiscuity, there is comfort in the words "The King has one more move!"

To those who think that the future of the world can be only disaster, the words ring triumphantly: "The King has one more move!"

And to the pastor, whose church seems to be torn apart with tensions and conflicting theologies, there is the good news—*the King has one more move!*

2

ANYONE FOR CALVARY?

A businessman commuted daily to work from his home in suburban Chicago. Every day, on the way home, a conductor would shout to the passengers, "Next stop is Calvary! Anybody for Calvary?" Calvary was a town that long ago had been left behind. Nobody seemed to live there. Looking out the window, the businessman saw broken-down houses and dirty streets. No one ever got off at Calvary.

Then one day, when the conductor asked if there was anyone for Calvary, a man stood and gathered his belongings to get off the train. The businessman was amazed. He didn't think anyone lived in this town that had looked dead for so many years.

The passenger got off the train and walked past the battered, beaten buildings, and then beyond them. The businessman, looking out the window, saw that there was a house up on a hill with lights on the porch. And, standing on the porch were three little girls waiting for their father to come home.

The businessman realized his mistake. There was another side to Calvary. He had always looked in the wrong direction. He had seen only the dirt, the darkness and the death of the town. He hadn't seen the other side where there was life and vitality and a loving family waiting to express its love.

So many people are acquainted only with the dead side of Calvary. They are filled with darkness and despair, and do not lift their eyes to see light and love.

3

THE PRODIGAL'S
FATHER

In England, a friend of mine wanted to set up a ministry in the nightclub scene in Newcastle. He decided that he would first visit the nightclubs of that town, a whole array of which were located in one area close to the train station. In each of these nightclubs there was a wild scene of intense music, flashing strobe lights, and bodies vibrating to rock music.

The fourth nightclub he visited seemed to be a replica of the previous three, except for one thing. Sitting off in the corner was a middle-aged man wearing a tweed jacket and tie. If ever there was a misplaced person, this particular gentleman fit the bill. My friend went over to him and, with a tone of amazement, asked, "What in the world are *you* doing here?"

The man answered, "Two months ago I had an argument with my daughter. She had gotten into drugs and become one of those strange young women who call themselves 'Goths.' She wore mostly black clothing, purple lipstick, and had dyed black hair. She was on drugs, and it was obvious, after she had stayed out all night time and time again, that she had become promiscuous. We had many arguments and one day a few weeks ago she stalked out of the house, slammed the door, and yelled that she was never coming back again.

"I know that she hangs out at places like this, so every Friday and Saturday night I come to this part of Newcastle to sit in a nightclub and hope that I will see her. I want to put my arms around her and tell her that I love her, and that any time that she wants to come home she will be more than welcome because I miss her so very, very much."

The fathers of prodigal children not only lived two thousand years ago. There are many of them in today's world.

4

GODLY MOTHERS
NEVER LOSE HOPE

I have a friend who is an alcoholic. Every Sunday, his mother goes to mass to pray for her son, that he might be able to bring his serious sickness under control.

One night, my friend and his drinking buddy were out until about three in the morning, hanging out at bars and getting very drunk. It was a rainy night and so cold that the rain was turning into ice as it hit the freezing pavement. The men were slipping and sliding along the streets when they came to the steep hill that led down to my friend's home. Both the street and the pavement were covered with a thick coat of ice. As the two men were trying to figure out how they could get down that very steep hill, his drinking buddy turned to my friend and said, "Well, your mom won't be coming up this hill this morning. Today's going to be one of those rare days when she doesn't go to mass to pray for you."

"You've got that right," my friend agreed, humored by the mere suggestion. But then, as they looked down the steep hill, to their stark amazement, they saw my friend's mother, crawling up the ice-covered sidewalk on her hands and knees.

Such is the love of a mother, especially a mother who believes that God answers prayer. Godly mothers never lose hope.

5

FAITHFUL PRAYERS

A few years back, I was the guest speaker in chapel at John Brown University in Arkansas. I had preached there on two other occasions and enjoyed a warm reception and good responses from the students.

On this particular day, as I was speaking in the packed-out chapel, I noticed a middle-aged couple sitting in the front row, listening with great intensity. Obviously, they were not students, nor did they appear to be part of the faculty. The two of them seemed to hang on my every word.

After the service was over, this couple came up to me and explained who they were and why they had come. Their daughter, who had been a student at John Brown, had been very difficult, rebelling against everything they believed and tried to teach her. She had become part of the Goth culture, cut her hair in a Mohawk style, worn only black clothes, and listened to depressing angry music that seemed to them to verge on the demonic. Worse than that, her behavior toward her parents was abominable. She seldom, if ever, said anything kind to them, and constantly sneered at their Christianity and mocked their Christian lifestyle. How she had ever ended up at this Christian school was beyond their understanding.

These parents told me that, because it was required of all students, their daughter had been at chapel when I last preached at John Brown. On that particular day, my message had been a very specific evangelistic message and when the invitation to accept Christ was given, she had made a decision.

After chapel, she had gone back to her dormitory and written a loving letter to her parents, begging for forgiveness for all the hurt she had inflicted upon them, and promising that, because Christ was now in her life, things were going to be different. The following weekend she promised to come home, just so they could be together and have a face-to-face reconciliation. It was a well-written and beautiful letter, and she mailed it that same day.

The next day, as this young girl attempted to cross a highway, she was hit by a tractor trailer and killed. The devastated mother and father buried their daughter, convinced that their prayers for her salvation had been in vain. Then, two days after the funeral, her incredible letter arrived. It could not alleviate the incredible sense of loss those parents experienced, but it did give them incredible comfort because they knew that their prayers for their daughter's salvation had been answered.

It was Yogi Berra, onetime manager of the New York Yankees and homespun philosopher, who said, "It ain't over 'til it's over!"

To that I would only add that, even when it seems to be over, the prayers of the faithful availeth much.

6

GOD CAN PUT ME TOGETHER AGAIN

My wife and I have made a decision that, when we die, we want our bodies to be used for science. First, we want the parts of our bodies, such as kidneys and the retinas of our eyes, to be removed and transplanted into the bodies of people who need them. Then, we want the rest of our bodies to be turned over to a medical school. We believe that medical students need cadavers in order to conduct effective scientific research and study. One day I asked my wife if she had any preference about what should be done with what was left. I asked her, "Peggy, do you want to be buried or cremated?"

With a smile, my wife answered, "Surprise me!"

Her reply was quite a contrast to my mother's words upon being told what we were going to do with our remains. I can still hear her saying, "But, Tony, on Judgment Day parts of your body will have been given away and different people will have them. If, in the end, parts of your body will be scattered all over the place, what's going to happen on resurrection morning?"

It was my turn for a little bit of humor and I said, "Mom, God is God, and God ought to be able to put me together again. After all, it was God who put me together in the first place!"

7

OTHER WORLDS
IN WHICH TO SING

A prominent speaker in the United Kingdom tells this story that carries us back to his boyhood. When he was six years old, his mother explained that if he ever needed help, he should dial "O" for Operator and ask for "Information." One day, when the boy's mother was away, his pet canary, which always sang for him, seemed to be sick and unable to sing. He remembered what his mother had told him, dialed "O" for Operator, asked for Information, and explained that his canary was ill. The operator, who happened to know a lot about canaries, gave him some very helpful advice and it was not long before the canary was singing again.

Thereafter, every time he was alone and needed help, the boy would dial "O" for Operator. Since he lived in a very small town, it was the same operator who answered each time. One day his canary died and the boy called the operator, who had become his friend, and asked if there was anything he could do to bring his canary back to life again. The kind woman simply comforted him and told the boy, "Remember this: there are other worlds in which to sing."

Years later, after the boy, now a young man, returned from his university studies, he remembered the kindly operator, and decided to call her again. A woman answered and he explained who he was, gave his name, and told how helpful her predecessor had been whenever he had needed help.

The woman said, "I was told by Mrs. Jones, the former operator, that someday you might call again. She told me about you when she was very, very sick. Mrs. Jones has passed away, but she told me that, if you ever called, I should tell you to remember that there are other worlds in which to sing. And she wanted you to know that what was true for your canary was also true for her."

8

JESUS IS MORE GRACIOUS

My wife loves to tell an apocryphal story about heaven. In Peggy's story, Peter is the keeper of the gates of heaven and keeps careful account of those who enter. The apostle Paul is the census taker of heaven, responsible for knowing how many people are there.

Peter and Paul are troubled because every time Paul checks the census against Peter's records, he finds that there are more people in heaven than Peter is letting in through the gates. Neither of them can figure out why this discrepancy exists.

Then one day, Paul comes running up to the gates, declaring, "Peter, it's not our fault! I figured it out! I know why there are more people in heaven than you are letting in through the gates! It's Jesus! He keeps sneaking people over the wall!"

That, of course, is the good news of the gospel. Jesus will allow into heaven many people whom the church, represented by Peter, would keep out. Jesus is more gracious than the custodians of the gates of heaven *and* some of our church leaders.

9

KNOWING WHERE
YOU ARE GOING

The great Albert Einstein was on a train leaving Princeton Junction in New Jersey, heading north. When the conductor came to his seat, Einstein was unable to find his ticket. He searched through all of his pockets and looked in his briefcase, becoming extremely disturbed. The conductor tried to comfort him, saying, "Dr. Einstein, don't worry about the ticket. I know who you are and you don't have to present your ticket to me. I trust that you purchased a ticket."

About twenty minutes later, the conductor came down the aisle of the train once again and saw Einstein, still searching wildly for the misplaced ticket. The conductor again said to him, "Dr. Einstein, please don't worry about the ticket. I know who you are!"

Einstein stood and said in a gruff voice, "Young man, I know who I am, but I am trying to find my ticket because I want to know where I am going!"

It's important that you know who you are. Your worth is established in relationship with Christ wherein you discover you are a child of God, and you are so loved that if you were the only person who ever lived God would have sent His Son into the world to die just for you. Furthermore, it's important to know where you are going, not only in this life, but when this life is over.

IO

A VERY SAD VERDICT

Robert Ingersoll was a prominent speaker on the Chautauqua circuit who gave many lectures on why he was an atheist. When he died, hundreds came to his funeral. Among them was his butler, who is said to have looked at the body of the great atheist and remarked, "Poor Bob, all dressed up and no place to go."

11

PHILOSOPHERS ARE KINGS

As a precocious schoolboy, William Temple, who was destined to become a great British theologian and one of the Anglican Church's most prominent bishops, asked his father, "Why don't philosophers rule the world, Father? Would it not be a good thing if they did?"

His father answered, emphatically, "They do—five hundred years after they are dead."

Why is it that the great moral philosophers have to die before they are heeded?

My conservative friends in the fundamentalist community often try to make the claim that they were always for civil rights, but the fact is that when Martin Luther King Jr. was alive, they defined him in demonic terms. Jesus reminded His disciples that people had stoned to death the prophets. Often, it is only after prophets are dead that the profundity of their messages is taken seriously.

Truth ultimately triumphs. God's people live with that hope.

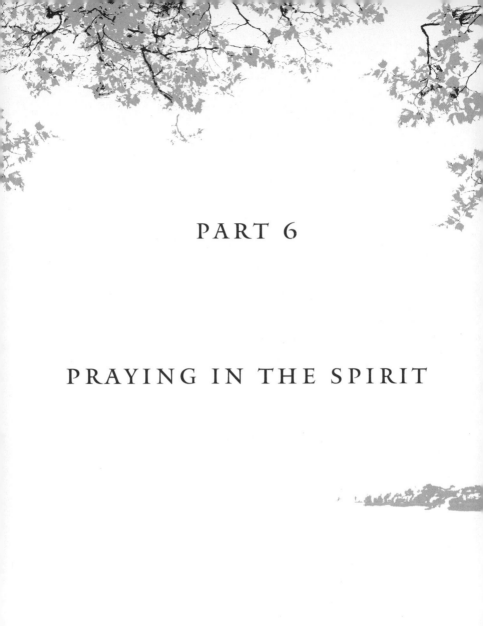

PART 6

PRAYING IN THE SPIRIT

PART 6

PRAYING IN THE SPIRIT

*Likewise the Spirit helps us in our weakness; for we do not know how to pray
as we ought, but that very Spirit intercedes with sighs too deep for words.
And God, who searches the heart, knows what is the mind of the Spirit,
because the Spirit intercedes for the saints according to the will of God.*
ROMANS 8:26-27

There is a special way to pray in which we let the Holy Spirit take
control of what we pray. Only then do our prayers transcend the
often-selfish desires of our hearts. When we allow the Spirit of God
to direct our praying, then the prayers that we ought to be praying
will fly to the throne of grace. Prayers that we, with our limita-
tions, could never put into words are uttered, as the Spirit prays
through us. More things are accomplished through this kind of
praying than this world can ever imagine.

I

GOD
LISTENS

One time, Mother Teresa was asked, "When you pray, what do you say to God?"

She answered, "I don't say anything. I listen!"

Then the interviewer asked, "What does God say to you?"

Mother Teresa answered, "God doesn't say anything. God listens." And then she added, "If you don't understand that, I can't explain it to you."

There are times of prayer during which nothing is said and nothing is heard. There are groanings in the depths of our being that cannot be uttered.

2

A CHALLENGE
FROM A TAOIST

While in graduate school, I had a Chinese professor who was a Taoist and had no belief in any god. One day, in the midst of a classroom lecture, he looked at me and said, "You Christians pray all wrong. You pray, 'If I should die before I wake' when you really should pray, 'If I should wake before I die.'"

The profundity of that statement has remained with me through the years as I have observed so many people who are half asleep when they should be awake.

In Christ, those of us who were dead are made alive.

3

SANTA CLAUS PRAYER

Sometimes we pray as if God is some kind of transcendental Santa Claus who promises to deliver the things that we want, providing that we're good and pray just right.

This was illustrated for me very clearly one evening when my six-year-old son came into the living room just before bedtime and announced, "I'm going to bed. I'm going to be praying. Anybody want anything?"

I am convinced that the understanding of prayer, of many of us who are older, often fails to transcend that of my young son, even though we may use more grown-up words to express it.

4

PRAYING PEOPLE
TO CHURCH

When I was head of the Department of Sociology at Eastern University, I used to take my senior seminar students to New York City for a weekend so that I could walk them around and help them to see and understand the dynamics of the city from a sociological perspective.

A church located in Brooklyn, just across the East River from Manhattan, gave us a place to stay on Saturday nights. We brought blankets and sleeping bags to sleep on the basement floor of the church. Sunday morning, we used the church kitchen to make ourselves breakfast, then, out of courtesy to the pastor and the church for their hospitality, all of us stayed for Sunday morning worship. The service was anything but inspiring. The choir sang off key and the preaching was dull, but we courteously sat through it all.

After a couple of years of visiting that church, I noticed that the congregation was growing. In spite of the bad music and the dull preaching, more and more people were showing up. I always tried to get my students to think about why this was so, and was delighted when, following the Sunday service, one of them asked the pastor the secret of the growing attendance at the worship services. He wanted to know just what the preacher was doing to bring in new people. The pastor replied, "This is Brooklyn and all around the church there are tall apartment buildings. You can't go in and knock on doors. The doormen wouldn't let that happen. There is no way I can visit the people who live in those apartments, but I do something else that seems to be working. Every morning at about ten o'clock, I take a folding chair to sit outside one of the apartment buildings and I pray intensely for each of the families that live in the building. When I can, I go up to the outside directories and get their names. Then, one by one, I pray for those people and those families. I do that for about an hour-and-a-half at the same building every day for a week, and I know that you're going to find this hard to believe, but on the following Sunday usually one or two families from that apartment building show up at church. When I ask them what brought them to this church, they seldom have a good answer. They usually say something like, 'I knew I needed church, and I have often passed by on my way home from work and thought that I ought to stop in and visit here some Sunday, but I never got around to it until this week. Something told me this week that I ought to stop procrastinating and come to worship here, and that's why I came.'"

The students were impressed and they began to sense something about the power of prayer. Later, as we mingled with the congregants outside the church, one of my students met a Puerto Rican woman and her two sons and tried to engage them in conversation. That mother had a very poor grasp of English and he enquired as to why she came to this particular church to hear a preacher who didn't speak in her primary language.

The woman explained, "Three months ago my older son was arrested by the police and put in jail on Ryker's Island. He gave us a call and told us that he didn't know why they had arrested him, nor did he know what would happen to him. He was frightened and crying. I didn't know what to do and a friend of mine said that the pastor at this church was always willing to help people, so I came to his office and told him what had happened. He dropped everything and went with me to the jail and asked if we could see my son. The man at the desk said that the policeman who was in charge of arranging visits wasn't there that morning and wouldn't be in for about four hours. The pastor told the man at the desk that we would wait.

"For four hours, the pastor sat there holding my hands, comforting me, and praying with me for my son. Later that afternoon, he got my son released and brought the two of us home. The next Sunday, the three of us got dressed up and came to church. We have come to church every Sunday since then. This is the only way we know how to thank the pastor for what he did for us."

Sometimes, the secret of church growth isn't anything the experts in the field can explain. Sometimes, it is praying and caring and doing for others what love requires that draws people in.

5

PRAYER IS PERSONAL

When I was in graduate school, I pastored two small American Baptist Churches in New Jersey. Not only did this give me a great opportunity to do Kingdom work with Christian people, but my salary helped my wife and me as we tried to eke out a living during the early years of our marriage.

I loved being a pastor except for having to pray publicly. That never came easily to me. In the Baptist Church, it was an unwritten law that ministers should never read their prayers. Generally speaking, there was a sense that to read prayers was somehow unspiritual. I was sure that if I ever did so, someone would be apt to mumble, "Oh, he *reads* his prayers! Did you notice? He *reads* his prayers!"

This meant that I had to make up the pastoral prayers right there, on the spot. I found it hard to connect spiritually and emotionally with Jesus and to be aware of the listening people in the congregation at the same time. There were times when I would forget the congregation and just lose myself in intensive connectedness with God, and often at such times, my street language from West Philadelphia would surface.

One Sunday, on the way out of church, a woman said to me, "Reverend, do you know how many grammatical errors you made in the prayer this morning?"

Before I could catch myself, I shot back, "I wasn't talking to you anyway!"

That was not a good way for me to behave, but there is something very, very personal about prayer. Jesus said, in the Sermon on the Mount, that public praying has its place, but if you really want to pray, you should "go into a closet and shut the door, and the God who meets you in secret will reward you openly" (Matt. 5–7, paraphrased).

6

ON ANSWERED PRAYER

A friend of mine told of attending a prayer meeting where people shared with each other about how God could answer prayer. One elderly missionary told how she had gone to the mission field wanting very much to be married. The other missionaries who worked with her were all married and had good companionship. She had longed for the same companionship these couples enjoyed. She had prayed long and hard for a husband. She concluded by saying that God had answered her prayer.

Out of curiosity, one of the women in the group inquired, "But why is it that you never got married?" The elderly missionary woman smiled as she answered, "Somewhere there is a 70-year-old man who has been fighting the will of God for 50 years!"

7

PRAYER FOR
THE CITY

Mike Yaconelli, one of the key leaders in developing youth ministries in America, once told me about finishing up an evening of meetings in Nashville, Tennessee, just before Billy Graham was to conduct an evangelistic crusade there.

It was a rainy, foggy night as Mike and a friend were driving back to their hotel. Driving past the steps of a building constructed to look like the Parthenon, they noticed a man sitting on the steps, his head between his knees, and his coat pulled over his head to keep out the cold rain and the wind. The man looked so pathetic that Mike stopped his car, and he and his friend got out and climbed the steps to where this sorry figure was huddled. Thinking him to be a homeless man, Mike said, "Hey, mister, you don't have to sit here in the rain like this. We've got enough money to put you up in a hotel. Come on with us. We'll provide what you need for a good night's sleep."

The man looked up, and Mike was shocked to realize that the one whom they had thought to be a pathetic derelict was none other than the great Billy Graham himself. "It's okay," replied the evangelist. "I just want to sit here for a while and pray for this city."

Mike and his friend retreated back to the car, and just sat there for a long moment. Then Mike said, "So that's it. That's why Billy Graham is able to win so many people to Christ. That's why he's so effective in the pulpit. Before he ever preaches, he prays over the city, just like Jesus once prayed over Jerusalem."

8

PRAYER REALLY DOES CHANGE THINGS

In various places across the United States, religious entrepreneurs sponsor "Jesus Festivals," where tens of thousands of young people come together to camp out and enjoy listening to their favorite Christian bands and singers. These events are kind of like Christian mini-Woodstocks. Interspersed with the music, there are usually speakers, though to many in the audience, a speaker is nothing more than a filler to give one band time to dismantle their equipment and the next band time to set up their equipment.

It was at such a festival that I had been asked to preach. The band that preceded me had whipped the crowd into a frenzy. Thousands of kids were jumping up and down, shouting and screaming, and waving their hands in the air. When the band finished playing, without much of a pause, I was introduced.

To say that the audience was uninterested in hearing an old guy like me belt out a gospel message would be an understatement. As I tried my best to preach, it seemed as though no one was listening. There must have been thousands of conversations going on, and people milling around all over the place. It was a tough situation that seemed as if it would defy any preacher's attempt to get the attention of the crowd, but I was there and I had to do something.

Instead of beginning the prepared talk that I had carefully constructed with illustrations and jokes that I thought would entertain the young people and keep them focused on what I had to say, I simply said within myself, *Nothing is gonna happen here today, but when I put my head on the pillow tonight, at least I will be able to say that I outlined, clearly and faithfully, the way of salvation.* Without illustrations, without any attempt to be interesting, I went through the reasons why these young people had to surrender their lives to Christ and what Christ would do for them if they did.

As my message wore on, I sensed something strange happening. A stillness fell over the crowd and, after about five or ten minutes, I realized that as many as twenty thousand young people were standing in rapt attention. They were focused on my words, listening with great intensity.

When I finished the message, I gave an invitation for young people to come forward to indicate that they were making decisions for Christ and to ask Him to transform them into new persons. It was one of the most effective invitations I have ever given. Hundreds of teenagers came forward. After a prayer, I directed them over to the huge tent where about twenty counselors were waiting to speak and pray individually with each of these would-be converts. These counselors were overwhelmed by the number of young people that came. I went over to the tent, called for attention, and told all those "seekers" that, if they wanted prayer, they would have to be patient and wait their turns because the number of counselors was limited. Then, I joined the counselors to help out.

I had finished my sermon at 9:30 that evening, but it wasn't until after 1:00 A.M. that the counselors and I ministered to the last of those young people.

Back at my hotel, totally exhausted, I fell into a deep sleep until about 8:00 A.M. At 9:00 A.M., I was picked up to go to the airport, but I asked to stop by the festival on the way. In the green room, everyone was buzzing about the awesome response to the preaching of the gospel the night before. I couldn't figure out why the message had been so effective, so I began to ask around as to what I had said that had stilled the commotion, caught people's attention, and made them attentive to the message. The sponsor of the festival replied, "To tell the truth, Tony, I didn't hear anything you said. When you got up to speak, there was so much noise and confusion that I simply stopped everything and prayed for you, that you would be able to get through it and that somehow the gospel would be shared with all those young people."

I asked another person and then another, and still another. Over and over again, I got pretty much the same response, "I'm sorry, but I don't remember listening to you. The situation was so chaotic last night that I just bowed my head and prayed for you, and prayed that God would still the crowd and make them attentive." I was puzzled and, to be honest, even a little disappointed, and then it dawned on me. It wasn't my preaching, but the prayers of all these people that changed everything. A couple dozen people calling out to God to still the crowd and make them receptive to a simple presentation of the gospel had done what all my planned homiletic tricks of the trade would not have been able to accomplish. In the words of Scripture, "The effectual fervent prayer of a righteous man availeth much" (Jas. 5:16, *KJV*).

9

HEALING OF THE SOUL

It was a dozen or so years ago that I was speaking at a Christian leaders' conference in South Africa. The other speaker was a preacher named Randy Clark who undoubtedly had spiritual gifts that were truly amazing.

One morning when we were at breakfast, Randy asked me if I had a healing ministry. I responded by saying, "If you mean, do I pray for people when they are sick, the answer is yes, but to be perfectly honest, not much happens. But if you mean, do I conduct healing services like some of those televangelists do, the answer is no."

"Why not?" Randy asked. To this I responded, "Because, as I told you, nothing much happens when I pray for people to be healed."

With a smirk on his face, he said, "That hasn't kept you from preaching."

A couple of weeks later, I was in a Nazarene Church in Oregon. As I got up to speak, I noticed that there was a little bottle of olive oil on the ledge inside the pulpit. As soon as I saw it, I felt compelled to say to the congregation, "There is some oil here. If any of you would like to stay behind for a healing service, feel free to do so.

"But first, there are a couple of things I need to tell you. First, I can't be in a hurry. I will need to connect with each one of you, to talk with you and get a feel for what you are going through. That will probably mean taking at least a few minutes with each person who stays for healing. The second thing is that, to be honest, I am not a healer and I don't expect much to happen."

About thirty people came forward at the end of the service and sat in the first couple of pews, waiting for prayer. I prayed with each of them. To my surprise, most of them had nothing physically wrong with them. Depression was the major reason most of them came forward for prayer. Just a handful of them had serious physical ailments.

Two weeks later, I received a telephone call from a woman who told me that her husband had been one of those who came forward for prayer. She then went on to say that he had had cancer. When I heard the word "had," I was thrilled. "Had cancer?" I asked. "How is he now?"

"He died," was her response.

I didn't know what to say. I apologized. I said I was sorry. I stammered a bit.

Then she surprised me by saying, "I really called to thank you. Before that healing service, my husband was filled with anger against God and against everyone else. He was only 58 years old. He had hoped to see his grandchildren grow up. He would lie in bed and curse God. Nobody wanted to be around him, least of all me. But after you prayed, everything changed. The last two weeks we had together was the best time we ever had. We sang together and laughed together, and shared a time of incredible joy. If I had a choice between those last days and our last five years together, it would be no choice at all. Those last few days were so wonderful."

Then she said something profound, "He wasn't cured, but he was healed."

I thought about that for a long time. Any cure is only temporary. No matter what miracle takes place wherein God intercedes and cures someone of something that the doctors said was incurable, the reality is that eventually the person will die. Cures are only for a time, but the healing of the heart, the mind and the soul is forever.

10

HEALING THROUGH FORGIVENESS

Dan Fountain served for many years as an American Baptist missionary doctor in Africa. He was there when the AIDS pandemic broke out and his clinic was soon overwhelmed with women who had been afflicted by the disease. At that time, the anti-viral medicines that can retard the progress of the disease were not widely available. Furthermore, even if they had been available, the cost of these medicines would have been prohibitive for any of the women who came to his clinic. In most cases, these women had become HIV-positive because of philandering husbands who had brought the disease home. In many cases, these infected women had given birth to children who also would become the victims of AIDS. These women were not only sick and frightened, but also they were extremely angry at their husbands, which is more than understandable. Many of them knew that they would soon be dead, leaving the children they loved without anyone to care for them adequately or provide for them.

Dr. Fountain wasn't able to do much to solve their medical problems, but being a Christian missionary, he cared about more than just their physical ailments. He was concerned about the anger boiling within them. In response, he set up Bible studies and prayer groups to deal with the whole issue of anger, and he did his best to teach these women how to forgive and what Jesus had to say about forgiveness. He taught them how to find peace of mind and heart through prayer, and how to be empowered by the Holy Spirit to forgive the husbands who had brought havoc into their lives.

To his surprise, Dr. Fountain saw some amazing results from these prayer and Bible study groups. He realized that, as a woman learned to forgive, the progress of her disease was slowed dramatically. No cures occurred, but when the women became able to forgive and to love through the power of the Holy Spirit, certain chemical enzymes secreted by their brains had a powerful effect on the disease they were fighting.

This led to Dr. Fountain's presentation of a paper at a major medical association meeting, explaining how loving forgiveness nurtured by prayer had a similar effect to the antiviral medicines the women in Africa could not afford. Prayer is effective in more ways than we know, and sometimes those effects can be measured scientifically.

11

WHY DOESN'T GOD DELIVER US?

A homeless man went by the name of "Tiger." He was homeless by his own choice because he refused to avail himself of any of the housing options that were offered to him by the church or by the government.

At night, Tiger would come and sleep under the portico in front of the church that my friend pastored. From time to time, he would come into the pastor's office to sit and chat with the pastor, relating his life experiences and trying to share his philosophy of life. Tiger was often depressed and on several occasions he had come close to committing suicide, but each time he gave up the idea because, as he said, "The Lord told me not to do it!"

One day, Tiger came into the pastor's office and declared that the night before he had been so depressed he had almost jumped off the bridge and cast himself into the river that ran through the middle of the city. "That's the place where I often go when I'm thinking about killing myself," he explained. "But just like the other times, at the last minute God said, 'Don't do it.' And I didn't."

My pastor friend said, "God told you not to do it because God loves you. That's why God told you what He did."

"Preacher!" responded Tiger, "If God wants to keep me from jumping off that bridge, why doesn't He change the things that make me want to jump? That's what I want to know. Why doesn't God change the things that make me want to jump?"

Most of us, when we are driven to the depths of despair, ask, like Tiger, why God doesn't deliver us from those things that push us to the edge. Why doesn't God intercede and make things different?

Many years ago, the Old Testament prophet, Habakkuk, asked the same questions. Then, somehow, through prayer, Habakkuk discovered a source that lifted his heart in spite of the existential circumstances of his life. He prayed:

> Although the fig tree shall not blossom, neither shall fruit be in the vines; the labour of the olive shall fail, and the fields shall yield no meat; the flock shall be cut off from the fold, and there shall be no herd in the stalls: Yet will I rejoice in the LORD, I will joy in the God of my salvation (Hab. 3:17-18, *KJV*).

PART 7

GOD'S PLAN FOR US

PART 7

GOD'S PLAN FOR US

We know that all things work together for good for those who love God,
who are called according to his purpose. For those whom he foreknew he
also predestined to be conformed to the image of his Son, in order that he
might be the firstborn within a large family. And those whom he predes-
tined he also called; and those whom he called he also justified; and those
whom he justified he also glorified.
ROMANS 8:28-30

Each of us is here by divine appointment. God looks upon each
and every person as a parent looks on a growing child, and is filled
with specific hopes and plans for each of us. Every person is viewed
by God as a unique creation with a special calling.

There is something special that God wants to do through you.
There is some specific good that God wills for each person who is
brought into the world, and if you do not do the good that you
were ordained to do, something wonderful will be left undone.
Your calling may not be to do something great in the eyes of the
world, but what the world calls little is great if God is in it.

I

YOU WERE ONCE A SPERM

When speaking to young people, I always enjoy telling them, "Do you realize you were once a sperm? That's right. You were once a sperm, and you were one of five million sperm all together in a group. Do you remember? All of you lined up at a starting line and at the end of a long, long tunnel, there was one egg. There was a race, and you won! Stop to think about that. The odds were five million to one and you came through. Your victory makes an Olympic gold medal look like nothing by comparison! You came through! You're a winner! You are here by divine appointment. You are no accident. Think about it. If your mother had had a headache that night, you wouldn't even exist. *You are a very special person!*"

2

WAKING UP THE CHURCH

Steve Chalke, a British friend of mine, preaches eloquently about the need to stir up the church to change the world. Often he creates a make-believe image of a raging fire and a group of firemen lying nearby, sound asleep. A young man comes along with a bucket of water. He looks at the raging inferno and then at the sleeping firemen. He can do one of two things. He can throw the water in his bucket onto the flames, but that wouldn't accomplish very much. Even if he kept on running back to the water faucet to fill up his bucket again and again, he alone could not put out the fire. On the other hand, he could take that bucket of water and throw it on the firemen, waking them up so that they could join him in the task of putting out the flames. It's obvious that the second course of action is the better one.

It is time now, to wake up the church so that together we, the people of God, can preach the message of salvation and attack the social problems that are consuming the poor and the oppressed of the world. There are those who do not fully understand that the church was created to be a movement to do God's work in the world. There is little question that it has to wake up to this mission, because too often we have made the church into a sleeping, self-perpetuating institution.

3

OLD AGE AND MONEY

In New York City, a woman driving a huge Cadillac came upon one of the rare parking places to be found along the streets of that city. Just as she was about to back in, a young man in a sports car whipped in from behind her and claimed the spot for himself. Then he leaned out his window, and yelled at the woman, "Youth and agility!"

The woman put her car into reverse, stepped on the pedal and bashed into the sports car. She then yelled at the young man, "Old age and money!"

Often, older people have money and can do things that younger people can't do. Their support is needed for missionary service. Old age and money have much to contribute to the cause of the Kingdom. Enabling young people to carry out their callings can itself be a calling. How many young people do not get to the mission field because they are not provided with the resources to send them that older people could easily supply?

4

UP TO A POINT

A young man was dragged into my office and shoved into a chair by his father, who let me know in no uncertain terms how unhappy he was with the way his son had turned out. "I sent him to college to get a good education, to make something of himself, and people like you got his head turned around. Look at him now. He's doing mission work. He's out on the streets with pimps and whores and drug pushers. He's given away his money to poor old ladies. He's living like a pauper and all he cares about is reaching out to the losers of the world." Then the father said, "Don't get me wrong, Campolo, I don't mind being Christian—*up to a point!*"

Whenever I tell that story, there are always waves of snickering and laughter that go through the congregation, and then I have to remind my listeners, "Aren't we all that way? Aren't we all ready and willing to be Christians—*up to a point*? And shouldn't we all realize that if we want to be true followers of Jesus we will have to move beyond that point?"

5

SINGING IN AUSCHWITZ

After seeing the motion picture *Schindler's List*, I did a radio program on the subject of the persecution of the Jews, reminding my listening audience of the horrors of the Holocaust and the sufferings the Jews had endured because of the anti-Semitism that pervaded Germany during the time of Hitler's reign.

The day after the program aired, I got a call from a man who identified himself as a survivor of Auschwitz. He thanked me for my presentation and told me that once a month the survivors of Auschwitz who live in the Philadelphia area get together for a breakfast. He invited me to attend their next gathering and perhaps interview some of the people who had gone through that horrid ordeal.

I jumped at the opportunity and, on the appropriate day, met him in the back room of a firehouse near the Philadelphia Airport. A simple breakfast had been prepared for about twenty men and women who sat down to affirm the bonds that had been created between them because of their mutual suffering.

I asked one of the men if he cringed every time he heard someone with a German accent, and whether or not his experiences had made him into someone who hated Germans. He explained to me that he bore no hostility toward Germans. "I was just a boy when they loaded my father and me onto a train and shipped us off to the prison camp. We were in a boxcar, squeezed together so that we could hardly breathe. It was more than three days that we traveled on that train. It would stop and sometimes sit for hours and we had no food and no water. The stench of excrement and urine pervaded the air and I remember crying because my stomach hurt from lack of food. But twice during the night at stops along the way to Auschwitz, people sneaked out of the surrounding woods, came up to the boxcar, and slipped pieces of bread and cups of water through the boxcar slats. My gratitude for those kindnesses is still overwhelming and every time I hear someone with a German accent, I think to myself, 'This could be the child or the grandchild of one of those persons who reached out to me in my hour of need.' "

There were other stories to be told, and the two hours I spent with those Holocaust survivors were some of the most meaningful and powerful moments of my life. At the end of breakfast, everyone stood, got into a circle and held hands. What followed was amazing. Together these survivors, these victims of anti-Semitism, sang a happy song. They sang, "You are my sunshine, my only sunshine. You make me happy when skies are gray. You'll never know, dear, how much I love you. Please don't take my sunshine away."

When they finished singing, I asked the man next to me what that was all about. He told me that in the prison camp, at the start of every day, they always got in a circle, held hands and sang a happy song because it was one of the things that bolstered their spirits and helped them get through the day.

Such is the resilience of the human spirit! I sensed that God was at work in the lives of these people in ways that are beyond my comprehension. Something of God's will was being lived out through them.

6

THE TRAGEDY IN THE 'HOOD

For years, our inner-city missionary program has recruited scores of university students to come to Philadelphia to work and minister to boys and girls who live in the government housing projects. They run programs that include Bible reading, singing, games, and cultural enrichment programs for children in the mornings. In the evenings they run programs for teenagers that include sports, discussion groups, and a lot of personal evangelism.

One hot summer day, when the morning program for children had ended, the boys and girls went into the apartment buildings to get some lunch from their parents. One boy ran up to his third-floor apartment to find a man there, beating his mother, slapping her around, and yelling at her to give him some money. It was the mother's "boyfriend" who had a drug habit and wanted her welfare check to nurse his habit.

The child ran to the window and began to scream to our young workers below to get some help. Our workers knew what to do. They immediately called the police who seem to be omnipresent in this overpopulated housing project. They responded almost instantaneously, charged up the steps, barged through the door, and trapped the man in the apartment. There was no escape for him.

He was a two-time loser and must have been aware that if he were to be arrested again he would be put away for a long, long time. In desperation, he ran to the window and jumped out, probably not fully aware that he was on the third floor of the building. He landed on a laundry pole that went in his rear and came out his neck. Impaled on that laundry pole, he convulsed and shuddered for two or three minutes and then was dead.

As horrible as that scene was, what I find even more tragic was the group of more than forty children who stood around that pole watching the man die. The extremity of the tragedy was that it didn't upset them very much. Within a half-hour, after the body was removed by the ambulance squad, the children were back at play. You would think that children who had just witnessed this horrific event would be traumatized. I know that in the affluent suburbs these children would have been put into special grief counseling for days. Not so in this inner-city ghetto. These children had been hardened. They had seen too much death. They had witnessed drugs ravaging their families, turning their sisters into whores and their brothers into pimps and drug pushers. For them, tragedy was an everyday event. They had become used to it. Their hearts and minds had been hardened, and that, of course, was the saddest thing of all.

After that terrible day, several of the young people who worked with us committed their lives to urban ministry. They believed that God had called them to soften the hearts of such children by caring for them and loving them into the kingdom of God.

Sometimes it is in the midst of the tragic that we discern His calling.

7

SEEKING WHAT IS REAL

One of America's most prominent preachers, Fred Craddock, enjoys telling stories and I love the one about his uncle who rescued a greyhound dog from the racetrack. When their racing days are over, these dogs are usually put to death unless people adopt them as pets. These dogs make wonderful pets.

Fred said, "I visited my uncle one day and there was the dog that he had just adopted, lying in the middle of the floor playing with his kids. The kids were rolling around on the floor, hugging the dog; the dog was licking their faces, and they were all having a grand time."

Fred said, "I looked at that dog and I said, 'Dog, how come you're not racing anymore? Have you gotten too old?'"

The dog answered, "Nope, I'm still a pretty young dog. I'm still young enough to race."

So Fred said, "Dog, maybe you weren't winning races anymore. Is that why you're not racing?"

"Nope," said the dog, "I can still win races. I'm faster than most of the dogs out there at the track. I was winning right up until I stopped racing."

"Well, maybe you weren't making enough money for your master," Fred said.

"Oh, no," said the dog. "I was making a lot of money for my master."

"Then why did you stop racing?" asked Fred.

And the dog responded, "Because one day I realized that the rabbit I was chasing wasn't real."

Sadly, that's true for many people in this world. They are chasing rabbits that aren't real, but unlike that make-believe dog, they don't realize that their rabbits aren't real.

8

TESTIMONIES

Since my late teenage years, I have been a member of the Mount Carmel Baptist Church, an African-American congregation in West Philadelphia.

Once a year at my church, we have student recognition day. I remember one of those Sundays when more than twenty college and university students sat on the first two pews. The pastor looked at them and, with pride and great affection, called them one by one to come forward and tell the congregation what they were studying and what they hoped to become.

One young man said, "I'm studying at Harvard University and I am going to be a lawyer." Elderly grandmothers and grandfathers responded with delight, "My, my. Oh, yes. Thank You, Jesus."

Another student said, "I'm studying engineering at MIT." Again, there were cries of approval and the clapping of hands.

A young woman announced, "I am studying music at Juilliard," and I heard grandmothers and grandfathers all over that congregation saying, "Wonderful, wonderful. Good, good. Thank You, Jesus."

You may think you have heard great music, but you haven't heard the greatest music until you hear about forty or fifty grandmothers and grandfathers moaning and groaning the moans and groans of joy because their grandchildren are becoming what America never let them be.

Always, after all the students have finished their brief presentations and are sitting there "bright-eyed and bushy-tailed," the pastor gets up, looks right at them, and in a stern, loud voice, declares, "Children! You're gonna die! That's right. You're gonna die! You don't think you're gonna die. You can't even imagine dyin' right now, but one of these days they're gonna take you out to the cemetery, drop you in a hole, throw dirt in your face, and go back to the church and eat potato salad!

"When you were born, you were the only one who cried. Everybody else was happy. That's not what's important. Here's what's important. When you die, will you be the only one who's happy, and will everybody else cry? It depends on what you're livin' for. Are you tryin' to get titles: bachelors' degrees, masters' degrees, doctors' degrees? Is that what your life is all about? Collecting titles? Or is it about collecting testimonies?"

That's black preaching at its best. It's got rhythm. It's got music. It's got poetry. I can still hear my pastor saying it over and over again, "Titles or testimonies? Titles or testimonies?" And then he did what only a black preacher can do. He swept through the Bible in five minutes. White preachers can't do that. We get bogged down. This man swept from Genesis to Revelation in one majestic run of words. I can still hear him saying, "Pharaoh had the title: "Ruler of Egypt." Now that's a good title, but when it was over that's all Pharaoh had—a title. He had the title, but Moses had the testimonies!"

With greater power in his voice, my pastor went on, "There was Queen Jezebel. Good title—Queen. She was going to destroy Elijah the prophet of God, but when it was over, all Jezebel had was a title. She had the title—but Elijah had the testimonies!"

"Then there was King Darius. Good title—King. He threw Daniel into the Lion's den, but when it was over, all he had was the title. Darius had the title, but Daniel had . . ." And the congregation yelled back, "The testimonies!"

The pastor went on, rhythmically chanting, and the people responded with joy and clapped their hands. And I can still hear my pastor as he looked down at those two rows of young people, saying, "When it's all over for you, and they lay you in your grave, what will you have? Do you want a tombstone with all your titles or do you want people standing around your grave giving *testimonies* about how you loved them, how you cared for them in the name of Christ, and how you made a difference in their lives?"

"I wish for you both titles *and* testimonies, but if you have to make a choice—you go for the *testimonies*!"

9

THE COST OF
FOLLOWING JESUS

An academic colleague, who was on the faculty of West Chester University of Pennsylvania, invited me to come and explain to his students how Christianity could be a movement that would foster positive and radical social change. I welcomed the opportunity, and as I spoke to his students I tried to do so with convincing passion. I could sense that the students were being swayed by what I had to say. They were coming to see that Christianity could in fact be a primary means through which poverty, racism, sexism, homophobia, militarism, and a host of other evils could be overcome by people joined together in a movement inspired by Christ and infused by His Holy Spirit.

As I was doing my best to win over these somewhat secularized sociology students, my colleague, standing in the back of the auditorium, interrupted me and shouted out, loud and clear, "Tony! Tony! Be sure to tell them the cost! Tell them what it will cost them if they become the kind of Christians that Jesus expects them to be. Explain to them the sacrifices that they will have to make if they are to be true followers of Jesus."

I was stunned. He was so right. And as I spelled out the cost, I could see that the enthusiasm that had once reigned in the classroom withered away.

10

LOSING YOUR CALLING

A missionary organization that I helped to establish has an array of ministries in Haiti, the poorest country in the western hemisphere. From time to time, I used to take my students to Haiti so they could see firsthand our missionary efforts, and get a glimpse of the poverty that pervaded that country.

It was on one of those trips that I took some students to a medical center in the north of Haiti. The day we arrived, there was a long line of people waiting to be seen by the one doctor and two nurses there. Most of those in line were children. It was obvious that the limited medical staff would not be able to care for all of those who needed help, and at the end of the day, scores of them, mostly children, were turned away.

Charlie, one of my prize students, said, with an edge of determination in his voice, "Doc, I'm going to come back here as a doctor. You wait and see. I'm going to finish my studies, go on to medical school, and come back to this very place and be a doctor. I'm going to make my life count. I'm going to save some of these kids. I'm going to keep a lot of kids from dying."

I ran into Charlie a few years ago on the streets of New York. To his credit, he had become a doctor. The sad thing was the kind of doctor he had become. He was doing cosmetic surgery, but not the kind that makes sense, such as putting a broken face back together after someone has an automobile accident. Instead, he was doing the kind of cosmetic surgery that caters to a sexist culture that evaluates women by the shape of their breasts. He was doing implants.

Charlie told me that his life had gone well and that he belonged to a church and was giving money to many worthy causes. As he continued to brag about the good works he was doing, I stopped him, saying, "Charlie, stop! Please stop! Charlie, you had a vision. You had a dream. You were going to do something splendid with your life. You were going to rescue the perishing and care for the dying, and look at you, Charlie. You sold out your vision. You sold out your dream. For what? So that you can have a Jacuzzi and drive a Porsche? You're a sellout, Charlie. Dress it up any way you want, but you are a sellout."

Looking back on that encounter on the streets of New York, I feel a bit guilty. Perhaps I was too hard on that young man, but then again, I wasn't any harder on him than Jesus was on the rich young ruler as described in the tenth chapter of Mark.

II

THERE'S MORE TO LIFE THAN MONEY

When a group of students from Harvard came back to the school to celebrate the twenty-fifth anniversary of their graduation, the alumni association put together a booklet with photographs of the students and their comments about where their lives had taken them over the previous 25 years.

In one of those books, next to the picture of a handsome young man, were written the simple words, "Making ten million dollars before I was 40 didn't turn out to be as wonderful as I thought it was going to be."

You can't help wondering what he was trying to say in that simple statement.

12

FIND YOUR OWN
CALCUTTA

A woman went to see her pastor after being deserted by her husband who had left her for a younger woman. During the visit, she explained how emotionally devastated she was by the rejection. She told the pastor that her husband had left her with enough money to live comfortably for the rest of her life, but that she felt emotionally dead and feared that she would live for the rest of her days without any meaningful existence.

After much counseling, the pastor made a suggestion. He asked the woman whether it might not be a good idea, since she had the money to do so, to take a few months to go to Calcutta, India, and work with the sisters from the Missionaries of Charity and Mother Teresa. He explained that the people working with the dying poor of Calcutta always needed additional help and that perhaps, in serving others, she could find meaning for her own life.

The woman took the advice of her pastor, wrote what she thought was a good letter, sent it off to Mother Teresa, and then waited anxiously for a response. Weeks went by and she heard nothing. This troubled her because she had been told that Mother Teresa always answered her mail personally. Then one morning when she picked up the mail from the mailbox in front of her house, she saw a letter postmarked Calcutta, India, with her name and address handwritten on the envelope. She rushed into the house and tore it open to see what Mother Teresa had to say. She was stunned by what she read. The letter simply said, "Find your own Calcutta! Love, Mother Teresa."

The message was clear to this troubled woman. You don't have to travel halfway around the world to find people who are in need. Each of us can find a Calcutta close at hand where there are people who are dying, not necessarily from diseases or lack of food, but inwardly dying nevertheless. The message is that our own souls are made whole when we forget ourselves and reach out to meet the needs of those people around us who need our love and our care.

13

BEING A CATCHER
IN THE RYE

Many, many years ago, in my student days, I read *The Catcher in the Rye* by J. D. Salinger. The book is the story of a teenager who, having flunked out of school, is about to head home to New York City. Before he leaves, one of his teachers asks him about what he plans to do with the rest of his life. The young man answers that he wants to become a "catcher in the rye."

He then goes on to explain that he often has a dream, really a nightmare, in which he is standing at the edge of a cliff. Before him, as he faces away from the cliff, he sees scores of children wandering aimlessly through a field of rye. The rye has grown so high that it is over the children's heads and they cannot see where they are going. From time to time, a child wanders too close to the cliff and falls to destruction. In the dream, the student calls to the children to turn back, but they don't know which direction is "back." "I don't know what else to do except to stand at the edge of the cliff and catch as many of those kids as I can," he explains to the teacher. "I can't catch them all, but I can catch a few of them. And when I wake up, I always think to myself that when I grow up I want to be—a 'catcher in the rye.'"

I often reflect on that story because it expresses so well just what it is that drives so many of us who are concerned about what's happening to kids in this day and age. We want to save *all* the kids, but there are too many of them, and so we reach out and try to grab hold of as many of them as we can, to tell them about Christ, counsel them, be their friends, and keep them from falling into destruction. In a sense, there are many who think that the noblest calling in life is to be a "catcher in the rye."

14

BECOME INDISPENSABLE

Miguel de Unamuno, the Spanish writer and philosopher, often declared that it was the responsibility of every human being to become "indispensable"!

It is in light of that declaration that I tell about a former student of mine at Eastern University. She came into my office one day, all aglow because she had secured a job in the Abingdon School District, having just finished her training as a teacher. With great pride she told me, "There were at least 200 other applicants for the job and the school board in Abingdon chose me!"

I'm not sure that I did the right thing, because I deflated her enthusiasm by saying, "I think that's a shame."

Perplexed, she asked me, "Why?"

"Because the school district of Philadelphia is 300 teachers short this coming year. In these tough inner-city schools there is a desperate need for teachers. If you hadn't accepted the job in Abingdon, there were at least 199 other qualified candidates who could have taken your place, but in Philadelphia the need is so desperate that there are teaching positions unfilled because no one has applied for them. Why would you go where there are others who could have taken your place, instead of going where you are desperately needed, where you could have become indispensable?"

15

ABUNDANT GRACE

Foy Valentine, professor of social ethics at a Baptist theological seminary, in his younger years, once spent a summer working at Koinonia Farms in Americus, Georgia. Koinonia Farms was founded by Clarence Jordan during the very early stages of the Civil Rights Movement. It was a place where African-American people and white people came to live and work together, sent their children to learn together at a little school that they had established, and fellowshipped with each other—all in an effort to demonstrate to those who lived throughout the South that black people and white people could live together as brothers and sisters in the context of Christian love. Koinonia Farms was designed to be a living demonstration of racial harmony nurtured by the power of the Holy Spirit.

Foy had a wonderful experience working at the farm for a whole summer, but when it was time for him to return to the university, he let Clarence Jordan know that he was very concerned because he didn't have enough money to pay for his tuition. At Koinonia Farms he had not been paid for the work he did, and though it had been a great experience and a wonderful time of spiritual development, his summer had not been economically profitable.

Hearing about young Valentine's dilemma, Jordon pulled out a check, put it in an envelope, and handed it to him, saying, "When you get back to school, open the envelope and perhaps what's in there will help you to meet your needs."

When Foy got back to his university, he opened the envelope and, to his amazement, there was a blank check and a little note that read, "Write in whatever you need."

The graciousness of Clarence Jordan is a reflection of the graciousness of God. So often those who are called according to God's purposes discover, in their times of need, that they are surprised with provision that fills them with joy.

16

CHOICES ARE IN OUR HANDS

In Chinese folklore, there is the story of a great teaching master who was so wise that he had the answers to almost all questions people asked him.

One day, some boys had a perverse plan to pose a question wherein the master was doomed to answer incorrectly.

"This is what I will do," said one of the boys. "I will conceal a little bird in my hands and then ask the master what I have in my hands. If he says, 'A bird,' I will ask him, 'Is the bird living or dead?' If he answers that the bird is dead, I will open my hands and let the bird fly away and, thus, show that he answered incorrectly. On the other hand, if he answers that the bird is alive, I will crush the bird and when I open my hands I will present to him a dead bird. Whatever he answers, I will be able to show that he is mistaken."

Then, this spiteful boy went to the master and did just as he had told his friends he would. He said to the master, "What do I have in my hand, Master?"

The master answered, "You have a bird."

"That is right," responded the boy. "Now, Master, tell me—is the bird alive or dead?"

The master answered, after long and thoughtful reflection, "The answer, my son, is in *your* hands!"

So it is for each of us as we are faced with the decision as to whether or not to yield to God's plans for our lives.

17

ALWAYS A
CHOICE

Clarence Jordan, the prominent civil rights leader and founder of
Koinonia Farms in Americus, Georgia, told of going to court with
a young man who had refused to report to the Selective Service
office when he was drafted during the years of the Vietnam War.

The young man was opposed to the war on moral grounds and
Clarence Jordan stood with him as he made his case to the judge.
He was eloquent and spoke with deep conviction and passion.

The judge was visibly moved by the young man's sincerity and
it was obvious that he wanted to be lenient. With great sympathy
he said, "I deeply appreciate your convictions and I recognize your
earnestness, but as a judge of this court I have no option but to . . ."

The young man shouted, "I have something to say, Judge!"

Clarence said, "I pulled the young man's arm and whispered
in his ear, 'Be quiet, he's going to go light on you if you behave
yourself.'"

The judge started to speak again and said, "I want you to know
that I have no choice but to . . ."

Again the young man shouted, "I have something to say,
Judge!"

Again the judge started to speak and again the young man interrupted. This time, he continued on to say, "Judge, you're going
to tell me that you have no choice. You *do* have a choice! *You can re-
sign!*"

There is always a choice, but sometimes the choices are hard
and the price to be paid for making the right choice is high.

I 8

HANDICAPS AS ASSETS

A dear friend, Dan Chun, who pastors the First Presbyterian Church of Honolulu, tells the story of a teenager who had lost his left arm in a horrendous automobile accident. The boy was extremely depressed. One day, the boy told his father that he would like to take judo lessons because it was possible to do judo with just one arm. The father, eager to do anything that might cheer up his son, quickly agreed and secured a sensei to instruct his son.

The young man went for lessons three times a week, and while he learned some basic judo movements, most of the time was concentrated on learning just one move. Time and time again, the training sessions focused on this one specific move that the judo teacher insisted that the boy learn perfectly.

After a couple months, the judo teacher announced to this young man that he was going to be entered into a tournament. The teenager responded with surprise. "Sensei," he exclaimed, "I've only been taking judo for a couple months. I only know one move very well, and I only have one arm. I don't think I'm ready for a tournament." But the sensei insisted.

The day of the tournament came and, to the young man's surprise, he made his way through the first round and then the second and the third round. He couldn't believe his success. What ultimately surprised him was that he made his way to the finals. Confronting the champion of the state, he was sure he was going to be destroyed, but to his amazement he not only survived but also was victorious.

On the drive home, the young man turned to his sensei and said, "I don't understand this, Sensei. I have been taking judo lessons only for a couple months. I only really know one move and I only have one arm. My left arm is gone and yet I just beat the state champion. I just won the tournament. Sensei, how is this possible?"

The sensei responded with great dignity, "You have won for two reasons. First, the one move that you do know well is the most effective move in all of judo. The second reason why you won is because the only defense against that move is to grab your opponent's *left arm*."

Jesus makes it clear that in our weaknesses, He finds strength. In short, what we consider to be liabilities and shortcomings can be turned into assets when we are yielded to the service of Christ.

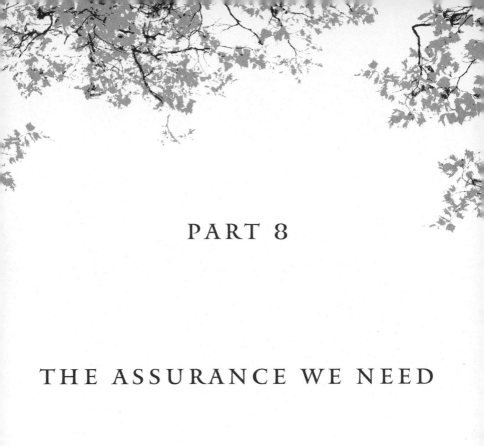

PART 8

THE ASSURANCE WE NEED

PART 8

THE ASSURANCE WE NEED

*There are times when we are buffeted with doubts about our salvation;
about whether or not we are loved and accepted; about what will happen
to us on the day of judgment; and whether or not we can have any
security about our relationship with God. At such times, these verses can
do much to allay those doubts and fears.*

*What then are we to say about these things? If God is for us,
who is against us? He who did not withhold his own Son, but gave him
up for all of us, will he not with him also give us everything else? Who will
bring any charge against God's elect? It is God who justifies. Who is to
condemn? It is Christ Jesus, who died, yes, who was raised, who is at the
right hand of God, who indeed intercedes for us. Who will separate us
from the love of Christ? Will hardship, or distress, or persecution, or
famine, or nakedness, or peril, or sword? As it is written, "For your sake
we are being killed all day long; we are accounted as sheep to be slaugh-
tered." No, in all these things we are more than conquerors through him
who loved us. For I am convinced that neither death, nor life, nor angels,
nor rulers, nor things present, nor things to come, nor powers, nor height,
nor depth, nor anything else in all creation, will be able to separate us
from the love of God in Christ Jesus our Lord.*
ROMANS 8:30-39

I

FAITH WITHOUT DOUBTS IS DEAD

Bono, the world famous rock singer, has become an icon to young people. His embracing of the poor of Africa in the name of Christ has inspired millions of young people to translate their Christianity into action by entering into the struggle to "Make Poverty History." Bono's Christian commitment is unquestioned, so it puzzled a friend of his when Bono released a song entitled "I Still Haven't Found What I'm Looking For." His friend wanted to know how Bono could make such a statement when he had come to know Christ in a very personal and transforming way.

"Doesn't your relationship with Christ answer the questions for which you have been seeking answers?" he asked.

"Oh, coming to know Christ didn't answer all my questions," responded Bono. "In reality, it raised a whole lot of new questions."

2

MEETING JESUS UNAWARES

My friend and one-time co-author Bishop Will Willimon told me about a time when he was the young pastor of a small rural Methodist Church in the south. One night, after an unusually difficult church business meeting, Will was out in front of the church changing the lettering on the church bulletin board. The congregants had all gone home and he stood there, alone and frustrated, as he changed the letters to spell out the title of the following Sunday's sermon.

As he worked in a dispirited fashion, Will looked up to see a strange-looking man standing next to him. The man appeared to be one of those homeless derelicts who often wander the streets of large cities, but who are seldom found on the back roads of rural communities. This particular man, wearing a worn-out old hat and a tattered suit, asked Will, "Are you the preacher here?"

Will answered, "Yes, I am."

His strange visitor then said, "I just stopped by to tell you not to be discouraged. You're doing a good job and I'm proud of you."

Will asked the man who he was and was taken aback when the man answered, "I'm Jesus." Then the strange visitor walked on down the road without any visible means of transportation waiting for him.

Will went into the parsonage next door to the church and said to his wife, "The strangest thing happened to me just a few minutes ago. A shabby old man came up to me and told me not to be discouraged and that I was doing a good job. And then, to top it off, he told me that he was Jesus."

His wife, quite seriously, answered, "And how do you know it wasn't Jesus?"

3

A FATHER'S ACCEPTANCE

The chaplain at a Christian college tells about a day that a terribly upset undergraduate came into his office for counseling. She sat in a chair in front of his desk, sobbing uncontrollably and holding her head in her hands in a posture of hopeless despair, as she explained that she had been "outed." "Some girls in the dormitory found out that I'm a lesbian and now the story has spread around the school. I think everybody knows, and the word is going to get back to my father. My father is a good man, but he is terribly legalistic and his literal reading of Scripture leaves no room for anything but condemnation of people like me. I know he's going to find out and when he does, I'm sure he will reject me. I love my father, and I'm certain that when he finds out I'm a lesbian he'll have nothing to do with me. I know I have to tell him because he's going to hear about it sooner or later. I just don't have the courage to tell him myself, and I don't know what to do," she finished, sobbing harder than ever.

The chaplain said, "You don't have to tell him. I'll tell him and I'm going to tell him right now." He picked up the telephone, dialed the father and waited as the phone rang in the church office. When the father answered, the chaplain explained, "I have your daughter here in my office. She is a wonderful Christian and she has served Christ so very well here at the college. She is the leader of the worship team for our chapel services; the hours she has spent tutoring inner-city kids is known to everyone here at the school. I could go on and on telling you what an exemplary young woman she is."

The father interrupted and said, "You're not telling me anything I don't already know. I'm proud of my daughter. When she is home during the summer, she works right along with me in the life of the church. She visits the elderly, she leads the youth programs, and her presence adds joy everywhere she goes."

The chaplain responded by saying, "Then we are agreed. Your daughter is a lovely person and a committed Christian—and in the next 30 seconds I am going to find out whether *you* are worthy to be called her father!"

Thus did grace challenge legalism.

The good news is that the father's legalism was no match for the chaplain's grace and he collapsed in tears as he said, "My daughter is my daughter. She is still a wonderful person and I want her to know that she will always have a place in my heart and in our church."

4

A MOTHER'S
LOVE

One night the phone rang at ten minutes after ten. The woman at the other end of the line said, "Dr. Campolo, I have a theological question to ask."

I must admit that I wasn't exactly thrilled with having to enter into a theological discussion over the telephone with someone I didn't even know after 10:00 at night. "What is it?" I asked in a gruff voice.

"When someone dies, is that person judged at that moment or do all of us stand before the judgment seat at exactly the same time? Are all of us judged by God on one single occasion?" was her question.

Tapping into my own understanding of the relativity of time, I tried to express the fact that, in all probability, we would all be judged at the same time. We would all stand at the same time before the Judgment seat and at the same time receive the judgment of God on our lives.

The woman said, "Thank you. That's a great relief to me."

I then responded by asking, "Madam, it's late at night. Why would you call me at this hour to ask a theological question of this nature? It seems like a strange question under any circumstances, but at this hour—why?"

The woman said, "My son was a homosexual and the church I belonged to spoke about gays and lesbians in such horrendous ways that he was driven to despair. Two weeks ago he committed suicide. The reason why I asked you that question was because I wanted to know if I would be able, on Judgment Day, to stand with my son before the Lord and then explain to the Lord what a wonderful and kind boy my son was. I just wanted to be there to speak on his behalf."

How much greater is God's love for each of us.

5

HUMOR IN THE FACE OF DEATH

A Catholic priest once told me about administering the last rites to a dear saint who had served the church and served his Lord faithfully for many, many years. As part of the prayers said over the dying man, the priest called upon him to "renounce Satan and all of his works."

The dying man, with a glint in his eye and a hint of a smile on his face, replied, "Father, I think that at a time like this I shouldn't offend anybody."

Together, they laughed. The man squeezed the priest's hands and slipped away into eternity. Those who are in Christ sometimes are able to laugh, even in the face of death, because those who die in Christ know that death has lost its sting and has no victory over the spirit of a trusting Christian.

6

CAN A BUDDHIST MONK BE "SAVED"?

Some years ago, one of the world's leading evangelical preachers told me about a visit he had made to a Chinese monastery. He had been invited to speak about Jesus to the Buddhist monks who lived in that monastery. After climbing a high hill, he entered the walled compound wherein the monks lived out their lives. As he entered the gate, he noticed off to his left one particular monk sitting in a lotus position in deep meditation. My evangelist friend sensed an impulse from the Holy Spirit to go over and share the gospel in a personal way with this particular man. With the help of his translator, he explained to the monk the gospel story. He opened the Scriptures and laid out the plan of salvation as it is recorded in God's Word.

As he spoke, the evangelist could see that the monk was deeply moved by his words. There were tears in the monk's eyes. My friend was so sure that the message had gotten through that he offered his hand to the monk and said, "Will you take my hand and pray with me, and in so doing invite Jesus into your life?"

The monk looked at him with a mixture of dismay and curiosity, then said, "*Invite Him into my life?* You don't understand. He is already in me. He has been in me for many years. I did not know His name, but even as you were reading from your book, His Spirit was speaking to my spirit and assuring me that everything you were saying was true. When you told me about how Jesus died on the cross to take the punishment for my sins, His Spirit affirmed that truth. I would accept Him," he went on to explain, "and gladly receive Him into my life, but He is already there. I am grateful for you because I did not know His name, nor did I have the details of His story until you came."

After telling me this story, my friend asked me, "Do you believe that Jesus was in that man before I ever got there, and that it was Jesus who convinced him that my message was true? And if Jesus was already in him before I arrived, what would have happened to that man had he died without me ever telling him the full story? Would he be lost throughout eternity? After all," said my evangelist friend, "the Bible says there is no other name given under heaven whereby a person can be saved. Just how important is it for someone to have the name right?"

Let us be careful, lest we answer these questions in a cavalier manner.

7

FISH
SYMBOL

Have you ever wondered why the fish, rather than the cross, was the earliest symbol of the Christian faith?

For the early Christians, the focus was on the resurrected Jesus. They were well aware that, when Jesus died on the cross, He took the punishment for their sins, but they were focused on the words of the apostle Paul, who wrote that if Christ had not risen from the dead, we would still be in our sin (see 1 Cor. 15:13). It was the *resurrected* Christ to whom they had surrendered their lives, and who had invaded and saturated their beings. The risen Christ was of decisive importance for them.

The fish, for the early Christians, was a sign of the resurrection. Jesus had told His disciples that even as Jonah was in the belly of the whale (which they understood to be a big fish) for three days and came out alive, so would He, after being dead for three days, come back from the grave (see Matt. 12:40). The fish—the empty fish—was the symbol of the resurrection for those early Christians. The empty fish was the symbol of an empty tomb; and the empty tomb was of paramount importance to the early church.

8

THE BATTLE HAS
ALREADY BEEN WON

Andrew Jackson, who was later to become the president of the United States, won fame as the general in the Battle of New Orleans, the last great battle of the War of 1812. Actually, that battle was fought, as you may remember from your high school days, when the war was already over. The peace treaty had been signed on December 24, 1814, but news traveled so slowly in those days that neither the British troops nor Andrew Jackson's army had received the word. So, in the early part of 1815, a deadly battle was fought and won by Jackson's army. If only he had known that the war was already over and that peace had been declared, what suffering could have been avoided. How many of us fight unnecessary battles?

9

CALLING BALLS
AND STRIKES

Three umpires were having a conversation. The first was a fundamentalist, and he said, "When I'm behind the plate, I calls 'em as I sees 'em." That's what you would expect from somebody who goes to the Scriptures and simply takes them at face value.

The second umpire was a theological liberal, and he said, "I calls 'em like they *are!*" Liberals always talk that way.

The third umpire was an existentialist, who responded by saying, "I calls 'em balls and strikes, but they are neither balls *nor* strikes until I calls 'em!"

God is present in our lives, but that only becomes reality for us if we *choose* to discern His presence and *decide* that He is always with us and will never forsake us.

10

ONLY ONE CHURCH

I was driving through the town of Mount Joy, Pennsylvania, looking for the church of God where I was scheduled to speak that evening, but I couldn't find it. Knowing that I needed help, I stopped at a gasoline station, where I asked the elderly attendant if he knew where the church of God was located and how to get there.

He answered in a slow drawl, "I knew that the Presbyterians had a church in this town, and I knew that the Methodists had a church in this town," and then, with a smirk on his face, he added, "but I wasn't aware that *God* had a church in this town."

Amused by his answer, I said, "It's been hard for me. There seems to be a church on every corner, but I can't find the church of God. How many churches are there in this town anyway?"

"There's really only *one!*" replied the sly old man. "I've been trying to convince the preachers of this town that there's really only one church, but I just can't get them to agree."

The old man was right! The time has come for all of us to face up to the fact that, despite our denominational differences, there really is only one church, which embraces *one* faith and *one* baptism.

Critics who mock us because they see those man-made differentials that separate us should stop and note how God unifies us in spite of our denominational differences. When we acknowledge our oneness, we have a shared conviction that God is with us and is working through us, and that all the demonic forces of the universe cannot prevail against us.

II

ENDURING UNTIL
THE END

After the victory of the Allied forces at the Battle of the Bulge, Winston Churchill was a guest at a dinner held in Westminster. The gentleman who introduced the British Prime Minister declared that the Battle of the Bulge proved, once and for all, that the British soldiers were braver than the Nazi soldiers and that was what had won the day.

When Churchill rose to speak, he started off by saying, "With great reluctance, I must challenge my honored colleague. The British soldiers were not braver than the Nazi soldiers. The difference was that the British soldiers were brave five minutes longer."

In times of doubt and when you are fearful about the future, remember to "hang in there!" Those who endure until the end shall be saved.

12

GETTING THE
WRONG MESSAGE

A little boy was taken by his father to an evening church service where the film *Martyrs of the Faith* was showing. It was a graphic presentation of Christians being thrown to the lions while the gleeful Romans cheered as the hapless believers were torn apart one after another. What made this scene particularly moving was that, instead of fighting off the lions or running from them, the Christians simply knelt in prayer and lifted their hands to heaven as they submitted to the terrible deaths.

The little boy, seated next to his father, began to cry uncontrollably. The father was very moved by this, believing that his son had been touched by the willingness of the Christians to suffer and even die because of their love for Jesus. "Why are you crying?" asked the father.

"Because that little baby lion isn't getting anything to eat," sobbed the boy.

There are times when each of us gets the wrong message—even from a very good story!

CONCLUSION

Stories, such as the ones you have just read, can serve a multiplicity of purposes, and I hope that this will be the case.

First and foremost, I trust they provided inspiration and insight for you, the reader. Perhaps they provided you with some new perspectives on familiar passages of Scripture and perhaps even enabled you to gain some good insights into how the Christian life should be lived. I hope that through some of the stories you read in this book, you have been led to reflect upon your own life, with all of its pros and cons, and to consider some new ways you might live out Christ's call to be one of His disciples.

Another desire of mine is that these stories will prove useful in your attempts to share the gospel with others. Stating the gospel in propositional fashion and spelling out the great and essential doctrines of the Christian faith, as important as that is, can sometimes come across as boring and hard for listeners to follow. Stories that illustrate what you are trying to say can help make your message clearer and go a long way to hold your listeners' attention. I personally use stories extensively in my preaching and teaching. One of my students once referred to my class as "Uncle Tony's Storytelling Hour." I gladly accepted that designation, but I went on to remind that same student that he seldom forgot the stories that I told him, and that with those stories, he would remember the points I was trying to make.

Many times people I meet in my travels tell me that their pastors have used some of my stories in sermons. I can't tell you how good that makes me feel. Sunday school teachers sometimes tell me that they have used my stories to spice up their lessons, and I'm thrilled to get those kinds of reports. I encourage the use of the stories found in this book for such important purposes.

I am sure that you have stories of your own that brilliantly illustrate the biblical message in ways that are relevant to situations in our modern, everyday lives. It would be a great favor to me if you would take the time to write them up and send them to me. Preaching as often as I do, I am constantly looking for new material.

Finally, remember me in prayer! I am getting old and I'm trying to get as much done as possible for Christ and His kingdom
before I "hang up my sneakers" and end the race that the Lord has
placed before me. Pray that I have the strength to carry on, and that,
in the days that lie ahead, I will live an increasingly consistent Christian life, and that I finish the course in a triumphant manner.

Pray for the ministries of the Evangelical Association for the
Promotion of Education, the missionary organization that I have
invested my life in helping to develop. Pray that these ministries
will go on blessing people—especially the poor and oppressed—for
years to come. There are a lot of very special people who have made
these ministries viable and effective, so be sure to pray for them
too. So many of the stories in this book have come from stories
that they have told me as they have worked with needy people in
very difficult places.

In the end, what is important will not be my sermons, or my
lectures, or my books. Instead, it will be the hundreds of young social workers and missionaries who have joined with me in the various outreach ministries of the Evangelical Association for the
Promotion of Education. You can learn about what they are doing
by going to www.tonycampolo.org and www.eape.org.

Thanks for reading this book. And if you tell some of the stories you have found in its pages to help others better understand
the "Ultimate Story," I will be more than rewarded. Remember that
history, in the end, is really "His Story" and it is this story that
must be told using every means possible.

ACKNOWLEDGMENTS

Authors write words, but those who take the words and turn them into books seldom get the credit that is their due. These acknowledgements hardly do justice to the work that these special people did to make this book possible. There is Jennifer Cullis, who did the proofreading, and then there is Sarah Blaisdell, who typed the manuscript and made a host of helpful suggestions. Mark Weising, the managing editor of Regal Publishing, deserves accolades for getting behind this effort and making sure this book got off the press. I would be amiss if I did not acknowledge my executive assistant, James Warren, who spent many, many hours coordinating all that goes with getting me to do my job. Finally, there is Peggy Campolo, my wife, who critiques everything I write and preaches to the end that I can do it better. She deserves my special thanks.

You would do my heart a lot of good if you would share your gem stories with me. If you email your story to my assistant, he will give your email to me. I assure you that as I use them, I will give you credit.

My address is:

Tony Campolo
Eastern University
1300 Eagle Road
St. Davids, PA 19087

My assistant's email address is:

jwarren@eastern.edu

INDEX